RECONCILIATION

RECONCILIATION

JOHN EDWARD JONES

WITH JOHN D. BONECK

BETHANY HOUSE PUBLISHERS

MINNEAPOLIS, MINNESOTA 55438

A Division of Bethany Fellowship, Inc.

Cover photo by B. B. Steel Photography
Typesetting by Type-O-Graphics

ISBN 0–87123–438–6

Published by Bethany House Publishers
A Division of Bethany Fellowship, Inc.
6820 Auto Club Road, Minneapolis, MN 55438

Printed in the United States of America

Library of Congress Cataloging in Publication Data

Jones, John Edward.
    Reconciliation: an attorney shows how broken
relationships can be restored.

    1. Reconciliation—Religious aspects—Christianity.
I. Boneck, John D.   II. Title.
BV4509.5.J65   1984   234'.5   84–9266
ISBN 0–87123–826–4 (pbk.)

Dedication

To my best friend
and wife—Carolyn

Contents

1

'You Picked a Fine Time to Leave Me...'

At 9:15 on a typical Florida spring day, my secretary interrupted some research I was doing on a pending case.

"There's a Mrs. Julia Houston to see you, John," she said matter-of-factly. "She says she needs your help."

Although I was busy, I was not *too* busy. I was an attorney, a Christian attorney, whose business it was to help people; without them, an attorney doesn't have a business.

People who came to me usually had major problems— broken marriages, serious injuries, or criminal dilemmas. As a lawyer I was trained to give them legal advice; as a Christian I was commanded to restore them in Christ's love. It seemed I was better at the former.

How could I really reconcile people who were so

broken physically, emotionally, and spiritually? I often prayed that God would give me the answer.

When I met Mrs. Houston that morning in the spring of 1974, I had no way of knowing that God was beginning to show me what He could do in my law practice.

My secretary ushered Mrs. Houston into my office, and the woman quickly told me what was wrong. "My son Kenny was arrested last night on some drug charges. He's in jail and is scheduled to appear before the judge this afternoon. We don't know what to do.

"We heard you are a Christian, and we're Christians too. Could you possibly help us?" she pleaded.

Julia spoke with a desperate urgency, although she was trying to remain calm. After asking her a few more questions, I agreed to handle her son's case.

I had worked as a criminal lawyer for four years when I was in the Navy Judge Advocate General Corps during the Vietnam War years. Since beginning a private practice, I had continued to handle some criminal cases. Because the vast majority of my military cases were for criminal offenses, I thought this young man's case would be rather routine.

That same afternoon her son was to come before the judge for his first appearance. I went to the county courthouse to be with him.

My strict Navy background had not prepared me for what I was about to encounter. Kenny was a long-haired, sloppy, somewhat dirty teenager. He was not exactly shipshape or military in his appearance.

As I gave him the quick once-over, I hoped my face did not reveal my shock. "Lord, what have I gotten myself into?" I thought.

Kenny and I chatted a bit and then went into the courtroom. "Your Honor, I represent Mr. Houston," I told the judge when our case was called. "I'm filing a formal notice of appearance and a motion for reduction of bond and release on his own recognizance."

The judge granted my motion. Kenny was temporarily freed while he awaited trial because he had no prior arrests or juvenile record, and his parents were stable, long-time residents of the county.

Because Kenny's parents couldn't be at the courthouse, it seemed there was no alternative but for me to bring Kenny back to my office until his parents could get him. Since they were both working and couldn't be reached by telephone, it looked like I was stuck with him—just what I needed with my busy schedule.

In the car Kenny and I talked more about his case and family. He had grown up in a home where rules were more dominant than love. He rebelled and chose the wrong friends.

He told me that when the police had stopped his car for a minor traffic violation in a small rural town, they had opened and searched the trunk without his consent or a search warrant. What the police discovered wasn't hay either; it was several pounds of marijuana.

We continued to talk about how the arrest and search were made and other aspects of the case.

Then, in the middle of our conversation, God spoke to my mind, "Why don't you tell him about Me?"

My mind immediately tried to dislodge the idea, and I argued back, "This kid is involved with drugs. He's rebellious. His hair is down to his shoulders. He actually smells after being in jail overnight. I think he should be cleaned up first and maybe taken to a church. Let a professional minister or counselor try to help him." That sounded like a good rational idea and got me "off the hook" while preserving my lawyer image.

But the Lord had other plans. "Tell him about Me," the Lord spoke to me again.

I wasn't quite ready to obey. As a Christian lawyer I wanted to help people, but I didn't want to impose my beliefs on others. It was easier to wear my Christian label as a "silent witness."

Often in the past, Christians who discovered I was one of them would say, "Oh, you're a Christian lawyer; that's so wonderful."

I got a nice warm feeling and replied, "Yes."

However, I knew that being a Christian lawyer was more than being recognized as a Christian. Christians should have something to offer people that will dramatically help them.

Finally, I glanced over at Kenny, and with my hand partially covering my mouth, I said, "Havyuhrdazezus?"

He glanced back at me and asked, "What did you say?"

"Have uu eveea acceeted jeesuu?"

"What did you say?" the young man asked again.

With an awkward gesture I pulled my hand down from my mouth and said, "How would you like to accept Jesus Christ? . . . I think that's the answer to your problem."

I expected him to say, "Don't try to lay that trip on me. I had enough of that Jesus stuff at home, and I don't want any more of it."

Instead, he said, "I'd like to."

As we pulled into the office parking lot and got out of the car, I was wondering, "Why did I open my big mouth; now what do I do?"

After entering my office, we sat down, and I told Kenny that God had a "wonderful plan" for his life. I actually fumbled through a "plan of salvation" booklet with him and was more nervous than if I had been doing an opening statement before a jury. By asking for Christ's forgiveness for his sins and by accepting Christ into his life to lead him, he would be a new person and God would forgive his sins, I explained.

Kenny closed his eyes and prayed simply for Jesus to forgive his sins and to be his Lord. His face brightened, and he became more relaxed.

I saw that he wasn't simply a "dirty hippie." He was a choice vessel. A rebellious young man had been reconciled to God by Jesus Christ.

The apostle Paul's words in 2 Corinthians 5:18 took on a very personal meaning: "All things are of God, who hath reconciled us to himself by Jesus Christ, and hath given to us the ministry of reconciliation."

In the days ahead God showed me how life-changing reconciliation could be.

Kenny had been an angry young man before. At home he had kicked holes in walls and doors. Because he was on drugs, his parents couldn't control him, and he often couldn't control himself.

There were many problems that would have to be straightened out in the Houston household. Kenny and his parents had suffered, and now there needed to be healing. I counseled both Kenny and his parents and saw reconciliation take place in the family. Love and acceptance formed in a home that just a short while before had fostered rebellion.

Still, however, Kenny had a possible felony conviction ahead of him. We all agreed in prayer for God's answer to this problem.

As I prepared the defense, I became convinced that Kenny's constitutional rights had been violated—an unreasonable search and seizure had taken place. I filed the proper motion with the court concerning the search and seizure, and the court agreed with our position and granted our motion.

All the evidence was suppressed, and the case was dismissed because the state could not prove its case. There was now no evidence left to support the charges.

I knew God had intervened and had used me as His instrument. He was giving Kenny a second chance. And Kenny took it.

In the following weeks Kenny's life continued to change. He took on a new friendliness and warmth. His rebellion was a thing of the past.

A short time later Kenny joined the Navy and continued to mature as a godly citizen. Out of 2,500 recruits at the Naval Training Command School, Kenny finished as the top recruit at graduation. His life had been transformed, and his parents proudly called all their friends to share the good news.

The experience with Kenny gave me hope. I knew God was interested in my practice and in the lives of my clients. I continued to ask the Lord how I could change from merely being a Christian lawyer to being His servant in all that I did.

I wanted to surrender my practice to Him, but it was a difficult process—three steps forward, two steps back.

To my natural mind it seemed impossible. As a partner in the law firm I felt a responsibility to the other five attorneys and to the staff in our office. I worried about covering the monthly overhead, which was substantial, let alone expanding the law practice.

Then, too, I had to make enough money to meet the needs of my own family. I knew God wanted me to take care of them first of all. How could I turn my practice over to Him? I might go broke.

And beyond all these considerations was the fact that I was a lawyer. I was aware of what many people thought of lawyers—even Christian lawyers. I knew the joke about the slightly inebriated fellow who made his way home on a cold autumn evening and turned left instead of turning right at a dimly lit corner. By chance he wandered into a cemetery and stumbled over a tombstone.

He lit a match to see what it was he had bumped into, and he read on the tombstone, "Here lies a Christian lawyer." The man pondered that for a moment and realized that he had to do something.

He looked for the home of a caretaker of the cemetery and staggered to the door. After knocking and waiting impatiently, the man heard the caretaker coming. When the door opened, the inebriated man spouted out, "Sir, you have a problem; there are two men buried in the same grave."

In my years of legal practice as a Christian attorney, many people, like that inebriated man in the story, wondered how it was possible for a Christian to be an attorney. I was still grappling with the same question.

My athletic, military, and legal backgrounds were in sharp contrast to Christ's direction to "love your neighbor as yourself" and "do good to your enemies." I had been taught to bury, or at least beat, the opposition. Lawyers aren't to reconcile; they are to win.

What if I chose to practice reconciliation more? I might have fewer cases. Fewer cases meant less money. I could reconcile myself right out of a job.

In the months that followed, I continued to handle criminal and personal injury cases, some real estate transactions, and divorce cases.

With divorce cases, however, I found myself increasingly frustrated. In the first years of my practice I had no restrictions on clients who wanted a divorce. I accepted either husband or wife and dealt with the dissolution of marriage.

During this same period, the divorce laws were undergoing radical changes. "No-fault" divorce laws were now superseding the older divorce laws. No longer was a divorce granted only on specific grounds, such as adultery; now divorces were being granted simply because of "irreconcilable differences."

I tried to be a good domestic attorney and rationalized my reasons for handling divorce cases by telling myself I had a chance to minister to those who were hurting. Divorce remains one of the most traumatic experiences a human can endure. In legally representing these clients, I convinced myself I was doing the right thing as a Christian lawyer.

"After all," I thought, "God loves everybody; He forgives everybody, so I will love and forgive them too."

But I kept stumbling across Mark 10:9, "What therefore God hath joined together let no man put asunder."

One thing attorneys are taught in law school and in the canons of professional ethics is that they have a primary duty to explore the possibility of reconciliation in marriages.

Although reconciliation is mentioned, it is not emphasized, and lawyers are not experts in counseling skills. Most attorneys do not make a serious attempt to reconcile marriage partners. They may quickly ask, "Do you think your marriage can be reconciled?" And when the client says no, the attorney guides the client through the divorce proceedings.

I wasn't like some other attorneys. I did want marriages to be reconciled. Realistically, though, when people reach the point of hiring attorneys, the chances for reconciliation are slim at best.

I knew what the Bible said about divorce. Malachi 2:16 says that God hates divorce, and I had read in Mark 10:5 that divorce had only been allowed because of the hardness of men's hearts.

Still, I wasn't a pastor or professional counselor. I was an attorney. People came to me for legal advice, not for spiritual help. I wanted reconciliation to be a normal function of my profession, but the odds appeared overwhelmingly against me.

Even if I could help a few people, divorce was becoming so accepted that I would be like the boy with his finger in the dike who wanted to hold back the ocean.

But God was about to teach me that all things are possible with Him.

One day a man came to me to discuss filing for divorce. He was a hard-working man with three children at home. He said that on the day before Valentine's Day he found a note on the door when he came home from work. "Dear Jim," it read, "I no longer love you. I have left home for good. Kevin and Jimmy are at the day-care center. I've taken Vicki with me. We've been married eleven years, and I think it's time for a change."

Jim's story reminded me of the song, "You Picked a Fine Time to Leave Me, Lucille." His wife had run off with the next-door neighbor.

As I listened to his story, I thought to myself, "This case is hopeless." I had handled other divorce cases, and I often thought they could be reconciled. But there was no hope for this marriage.

In other divorce cases I had seen a glimmer of hope. There was simply a breach of confidence or a financial problem or something else that could be worked out. But to my natural mind this divorce case was beyond repair.

Jim's minister, a modern, enlightened individual, didn't even consider this a theological question. He sent Jim to me for professional guidance.

I started explaining Jim's legal rights and the legalities of divorce proceedings.

As we talked, the Lord flashed a series of thoughts through my mind in an instant's time. "Share with this man about Jesus. Tell him about the miracle power of God. Give him hope. Let him know his marriage can be reconciled."

I was reluctant to verbalize these thoughts to Jim. My intellectual credibility and professional pride with a new client (referred by a prominent clergyman) were at stake. What should I do now?

With significant hesitation, I changed the subject from divorce to reconciliation. "I know you feel devastated, Jim," I said, "but I believe God can reconcile your marriage if you will give Him a chance."

I was taking a chance myself. I could just be giving him some false hopes that would only prolong his agony and complicate the divorce even further. But as I continued to talk to him, I knew the Holy Spirit was guiding our conversation.

I told him how much Jesus loved him and wanted their marriage to be whole. I had never been so spiritually candid with a divorce client before.

Jim's heart was open to what I said. He still loved his wife and wanted the marriage to work. However, he was afraid and wanted to be legally protected if his wife didn't return home.

I advised Jim of the legal consequences, and he decided to file a petition for dissolution to protect himself, his children, and the property. Even though his first choice was reconciliation, he still had fear and uncertainty.

Jim and I prayed for God to heal the marriage, and I asked God to help him forgive his wife. Jim left my office that day with different hopes than when he had come.

Over the next several months I worked closely with Jim. When a person is going through divorce proceedings, each day seems like an eternity. A day seems like a week and time becomes a blur—you begin to wonder when and if it will ever change or end.

Jim was going through these feelings, and I talked with him daily in person or on the phone. He wondered whether it was worth the risk; would prayer and reconciliation really work? With his engineering background he wanted to analyze exactly how everything would work.

I would listen and try to reassure him as he grew in his faith. God was working on Jim's heart and, to his surprise, on his wife's heart too. After several months, Jim's wife got enough courage to call and tell him she wanted to come back home.

Jim told his wife to come back. He was willing to take a risk. God had worked forgiveness in his heart.

When Jim and his wife were reunited, they had many problems to work out on a daily basis. But God helped them and ministered to both of their lives. They received competent spiritual and psychological counseling that opened their communication avenues.

They didn't simply co-exist either. A greater, more mature love blossomed in them, and God baptized them in the Holy Spirit.

Their marriage once again became whole and has continued to grow for the last eight years. They have been able to minister to others and take positions of responsibility in their local church during this time.

Through this incident, God had given me another dramatic example of His power to heal and reconcile. I began believing that nothing is too big for God if people will allow Him to work through their lives.

I vowed to God to be His minister of reconciliation; however, I did not realize how difficult it would be to keep my word. It called for a radical change—change that forced me to painfully re-examine the deepest motives and patterns that had developed from childhood.

2

Everybody Comes from Somewhere

I had learned a lot about vows as a boy growing up in the rural South. A young man was taught, "A gentleman is a man of his word," and, "Your word is your bond." It was a matter of honor about keeping one's word—no matter how difficult it was. Many times I wished that I had just kept my mouth shut in the first place.

My mother often told me, "It is better to keep your mouth shut and be thought a fool than to open your mouth and remove all doubt." But I was a slow learner.

I was born in Bainbridge, Georgia, because my home town of Colquitt did not have a hospital. Colquitt was a town of about 3,000, including everybody's dog and cat. It was so far off the mainstream that I often believed they pumped sunshine in. It was the type of place where if someone plugged in a toaster, the lights dimmed in neighboring houses.

It would be harder to describe except a peanut farmer from a neighboring town of Plains was elected President of the United States in 1976.

In our town it seemed everyone was either a Methodist or a Baptist. On Sundays people slept in or went to church, and some would do both simultaneously. Our preacher was fond of saying, "Blessed are they that blink, for they shall soon enter the land of Nod." He knew his congregation well, even if we never did find that exact quote in the Beatitudes.

I grew up in a Christian home and for the first eight years of my life enjoyed family security. My father held every important position possible in the community. He had been a Sunday school teacher and director; the county school superintendent; the high school principal; a Mason, Lion, Moose, and Elk. He was a big frog in our little pond, and I was unaware there was a great big ocean out there. I also didn't realize then that he was over-extended and rarely home with us.

As a child, I accepted Jesus into my heart, went forward in church, and made a public profession of faith. However, I was not taught how to apply the faith to the real problems of life. I became frustrated, hearing salvation and rededication messages repeated twice a week, fifty-two times a year. By the time I was a young man, I had rededicated my life so many times my rededicator had worn out.

Five days before my ninth birthday, I received a splash of reality in my life. I was curled up in my new double bed, listening to my mother read the comic strips on a warm spring night, when the telephone rang.

Mother told me to go to sleep and went to answer

the phone. Then mom ran to my room and said, "Your daddy's been in a serious car accident! I'm taking you to your grandmother's house and I'm going to the hospital."

I don't remember the trip to grandmother's, except for the feeling of total frustration and helplessness. I reached my grandmother's and sensed the near panic in the adults.

The mayor, one of the town doctors, and another prominent businessman were also injured in the auto wreck when a drunken driver plowed into their car. My grandmother told me to pray for my father.

As a small child my prayer was, "God, save my father; let him live. Amen."

After several hours which seemed like an eternity my mother came in and told me, "Daddy's dead." He died on the operating table.

While the other three men survived, I wondered, "God, where are You? What happened? Why?" No one around me had the answer to these questions.

Our entire house was full of flowers before the funeral, and many people came to pay their respects. But they couldn't answer my questions either—only ask more.

A friend of my father's asked about a large floral arrangement in the shape of a fish. "Do you ever think your father caught a fish that big?"

I assured him that daddy had.

Then he asked, "Do you think you will be able to fill your daddy's shoes?"

I didn't know for sure, but I was certainly going to try.

As I tried, my unanswered prayer lingered in my mind and shaped a belief that many people already held: God doesn't intervene in the lives of everyday people like me—maybe others, but not me. I often quoted and believed, "God helps those who help themselves." I was an adult before I realized the quote was from Ben Franklin instead of the Bible.

As I grew into a young man, I continued to be bombarded with more questions. I was searching for someone with answers, but all I heard was more questions.

At the family reunions each year the question was always the same, "How are you doing?"

I responded that I was doing fine, thank you, whether I was or not, because that was the expected answer.

The question was not asked to discover how I was feeling spiritually or emotionally; instead, it was a question that implied, "What kind of grades are you making? Where are you going to college? What job or profession will you have? How much money will you make?" Our family always went to the financial bottom line real fast. No one ever accused us of being unable to count.

I decided to answer the question exactly the way it was asked, with goal-setting and success at each stage of life. I was not going to get too serious about religion. After all, religion had not saved my father's life. I was going to get serious about my future in the here and now.

In my schooling I tried to emulate my father's reported perfection. My grades were always outstanding. Whatever I did was goal-centered, not God-centered. I tried to make me the best person I could and, for a long time, succeeded. My relatives in kindness told me of my father's accomplishments and not his disappointments and shortcomings. I often think it would be kinder to children if adults would be objective and honest about deceased parents or relatives. Somehow we confuse honesty with disrespect for the dead and simply omit certain things. So the surviving child tries to fulfill the image of perfection in the real world and fails. With each failure there is frustration and re-determination to try again to fulfill the dream.

During this period in my life my mother was my closest friend. She was mother and father to me and endured high school football, baseball, and track, plus hunting and fishing. She was a real pal—the kind who would yell at the referee and tell the other team to quit piling on her boy.

In high school I took virtually every course offered. I went to summer school because my mother returned to college for a graduate degree to better support us. In my senior year I actually had to take home economics because I'd taken everything else.

Since my mother was a college professor, there was little doubt that I was going to attend college. I didn't really think about it or know I had a choice. I simply looked at college as grades thirteen through sixteen. I started college two weeks after high school graduation.

In college I continued the same patterns I had followed in high school, wanting to excel in everything. I equated success with popularity and personal glory.

I attended Florida State University, still thinking I could do it all. I was in the English honors program, president of Sigma Alpha Epsilon fraternity, and a member in the Gold Key Honor Society and Omicron Delta Kappa leadership fraternity.

Then in my junior year I ran for student body president and won over two opponents. But I was not realistic about what one person could accomplish.

The patterns learned in childhood came tumbling down with a thud.

I was trying to be everything to everybody at the university and couldn't do it. I was over-extended and so were my ethics. Since I had the need for more success and approval, I made a costly miscalculation when I had a paper due in a creative writing class right after the election as student body president. At that point I was "burned out"—not creative. I was also unable to admit my own limitations. I took a shortcut. Not having enough time to do the work as it should have been done, I plagiarized from another source.

After I turned the assignment in, I knew I had made a mistake. I had just been sworn in as president of the student body and took an oath to uphold the student "honor system."

I realized the way the game was played that the professors had the "honor" and the students had the "system." Nevertheless, I couldn't live with myself. I turned myself in to the chief justice of the honor council.

My decision created quite a stir at the university. There were mixed reactions by different students and university officials. Some friends wondered why I was so naive or stupid to admit the violation. I went from student body president to college "kick-out" in a matter of weeks.

Now my whole future might be lost. I had some political ambitions and thought this mistake ended that personal goal.

Through this traumatic experience God began showing me some things about myself and my ambitions—although at the time I didn't realize He was trying to get my attention.

I saw that personal goals must not overpower absolute convictions. I was responsible to God and others for my actions; situational ethics were very shallow. There were still some absolute values in life.

I also discovered that I was not infallible. I made mistakes, and I couldn't run away from them. I found that I was a part of the human race—no better or worse—and was simply a person who had sinned and was in need of grace.

Some people advised me not to go back to the university. Some friends said I should tell the university to "stick it in their ear" and transfer to a different university.

I learned a lot about people through this difficult experience. While some people stood by me and gave me good advice, others were fair-weather friends who wanted to use me or my position as student body president to further themselves. When I fell from favor, they quickly left me.

However, one of the people who stood by me and confirmed my decision was my girlfriend Carolyn. She had absolute ethics and encouraged me, especially during periods of depression. Her faithfulness and integrity made her a good friend and, later, a loving wife.

During this time, too, I started reading the Bible once again as I had been trained to do when I was a child. But that urge diminished as the crisis passed. I wanted my own way more than God's way.

I decided to humble myself before the university and reapply. That was one of the hardest things I've ever had to do. I asked the dean of students for readmission and said I had learned a valuable lesson.

I had made a mistake, and I had paid for it. Now I

should be able to continue my life.

I thought I could correct my life's course by establishing clearer priorities. "If I can keep my life in balance," I told myself, "I'll still be able to achieve my goals."

Despite the lessons learned, I resumed my old ways of being number one. I was like the farmer who took his first trip on an airplane. About midway through the flight at about 35,000 feet the plane flew into some turbulent weather. The farmer nervously looked out the window at the engines and worried that they might fall off.

All at once the plane hit an air pocket and dropped about 4,000 feet in a matter of seconds. The panicked farmer cried out loud, "Lord, if You get me out of this, I'll give You half of everything I own."

A few seconds later the plane broke out of the storm and calmly continued to its destination.

After the flight a preacher approached the farmer as he waited to pick up his luggage. "I was sitting behind you in the plane and heard your promise to God," the preacher said. "I'm here to collect."

"I'm sorry. I made God a better offer," the farmer quickly replied. "The minute I put my feet back on the good earth, I promised God that if I ever flew in one of those planes again, He could have everything I owned."

When I got my own feet back on the ground I repeated old patterns. Once again I achieved an almost perfect academic record in my senior year. I was elected president of my social fraternity. At graduation I was named to the student "Hall of Fame" as one of the top graduates. I saw a rosy future for me and my wife-to-be.

Carolyn and I were married in August of 1965, and

that fall I enrolled in law school at Stetson University. My goals were not diminished; I was determined to be the best in the class and to achieve all the honors I could. I knew that the more honors I achieved now, the better my chances for getting a high-paying, successful job in the future. I ended up being president of the Phi Delta Phi legal fraternity, in the top five percent of my graduating class, and a Charles A. Dana Scholar. I became one of two graduates to become a law clerk to a federal judge after graduation in June of 1968.

So despite my setback in my junior year at Florida State University, I thought I was on my way to achieving my goals. How could I know a war in the little country of Vietnam—halfway around the world—could change so many people's lives?

One day I received a letter that began, "Greetings." I was informed that I was number one of the draft eligibility list—the only list I didn't want to be number one on.

I showed the letter to the federal judge for whom I was working, and he responded that getting a deferment should be no problem. He didn't know how the three-man draft board in Colquitt, Georgia, viewed federal judges and other things in life. The only thing the draft board knew about federal judges was that they sent black students to white schools, and the draft-board members weren't in favor of that.

Relatives back in Colquitt became very friendly with the draft-board members, hoping to obtain my deferment. Three U.S. Senators intervened in my behalf. I drove up to Colquitt myself and appeared before them in my three-piece lawyer's suit to plead my case.

The board was not impressed. They were three

farmers who had known me from my childhood. One draft-board member, who was wearing a light cotton jacket with a patch on it proclaiming, "Grow Vigoro," spoke to me. "Son," he said, "I've known you since you were knee-high to a grasshopper. Your grand-daddy served in World War I, your daddy served in World War II, and you're gonna be in this one."

I knew my draft board and I were not communicating.

I immediately set new goals. I saw that I wasn't going to be deferred as a law clerk, so I determined to be deferred as a member of the FBI.

I took and passed all the exams and entrance requirements for the FBI. The FBI sent an agent to my draft board, informing them of my future position. The FBI had told me this was a mere formality. No one had ever said no to J. Edgar Hoover before in a case like this. (The FBI did not know my local draft board.)

The same three men met with the FBI official. One of the draft-board members said he heard that the FBI was in need of typists and thought I didn't know how to type. Deferment denied.

I quickly considered my options. At the time, the Supreme Court had recently ruled that servicemen had the right to legal counsel. Consequently, the Navy was required to recruit some attorneys although they didn't want to.

I was accepted by the Navy in January of 1969 as a member of the Judge Advocate General Corps. The Navy greeted their new attorneys with the same enthusiasm that the Pharaoh of Egypt had greeted the plagues.

My goals had been side-tracked, but a temporary setback would not damage my future, I thought.

From the beginning I had planned to be a law clerk for a federal judge for two years. Next I would be an assistant United States Attorney for an additional two years. After that I was going to join a major law firm in their litigation department, and from there I would continue my career until retirement. I was the type of person who had life planned until at least age fifty-five. The Navy was simply a minor interruption to my long-range goals. I would spend the four years as a Navy lawyer and then continue my career plan.

But God had other plans.

I had set goals because I knew it was impossible to achieve anything without planning. But, quite frankly, my real motive for setting goals was to make myself secure. I couldn't stand the idea of being insecure or dependent on others. What really mattered to me was financial success, professional expertise, and popularity. I believed that money brought respect and success, and I wanted both.

During my career in the Navy I took on other responsibilities. On weekends I was a professional football scout for the Kansas City Chiefs. I also was an investigator for a personal-injury attorney. The goals I set to erase my insecurity dominated my life.

I even placed personal ambition ahead of having a happy marriage. I attended church with my wife but did not see much reality or spiritual application for my life. I sincerely tried but didn't feel I was receiving anything of real value.

And my relationship with Carolyn was shallow because I didn't communicate with her. I was more interested in my needs than in hers.

During our entire marriage, Carolyn had been attempting to improve our communication, marital relationship, and spiritual growth.

When I had tried to manipulate the draft board, she was suggesting prayer for God's guidance. I thought she was sweet and naive in these matters. I would handle the situation like a man—with my own intellect and ability—someone I could depend on, I thought.

When the Navy moved us to Corpus Christi, Texas, Carolyn continued her efforts to improve our marriage and her husband. One night we had dinner with Gene and Ellen, a couple we met at church. Before, during, and after dinner, we observed this couple communicate on a feeling level with depth. It was honest, open, and vulnerable sharing without pretense.

When we left their home, we knew they had something in their marriage which was lacking in ours, and we wanted it. We started meeting weekly with them and two other couples and began to learn more about ourselves and each other. We also learned to pray for each other. Because of this couple's insistence, we attended a Christian retreat at Laity Lodge in Leaky, Texas, with them in late 1969.

There I saw Christians who were also professionals but who were different from my stereotype of a professional. They were concerned with each other's feelings.

They had a love for Jesus and for each other that I hadn't experienced in my denominational background. From their example, I realized that my Christianity had only been in my mind and not in my heart. I wanted what they had. My goals didn't measure up to the joy and peace I saw in their lives. I asked Christ to change my life and be my Master. I transferred my ideas of God from my head to my heart, and when I did that, my life began to change.

For the first twenty-six years of my life I had tried

to make me number one. My way had left me insecure.

God had given me ample evidence from the past that my idea of the self-made man was on a shaky footing. It had cost me my reputation when I plagiarized in college. It had not worked when a three-man draft board decided my future.

Now I decided to try things God's way.

The first real test soon followed our experience at Laity Lodge. After two years in Corpus Christi, Texas, the Navy scheduled me for transfer. Carolyn and I wanted to return to Florida—especially Orlando. However, the Navy stated they had no intention of transferring me to my home state.

This time when Carolyn suggested we pray specifically about the move, I was ready (although a little skeptical about making specific requests). We prayed to be stationed at the Navy Training Center, Orlando—not Pensacola, Jacksonville, or Key West.

After several months, we received a telephone call and orders to Orlando. In July of 1971 we moved. God had answered our specific prayer, and our faith began to grow.

Still, some patterns are hard to break. I had tasted enough personal success to think I could continue in my new Christian walk by simply transferring my goal-setting patterns to my new life.

That, I was to discover, wouldn't work either.

3

Single-minded

After I accepted Jesus into my life, every problem I ever faced did not automatically disappear. I discovered that while Jesus was the answer to my problems, I didn't know how to apply the answer to many areas of my life.

I was still John Jones—complete with goals, insecurities, and hidden fears.

In my new spiritual life I quickly discovered the truth of James 1:8: "A double-minded man is unstable in all his ways."

In the coming years (even as God was showing me the beauty and importance of reconciliation in my personal life and law practice) I battled to have one goal—God's will.

Today's society puts so many demands on professionals and businessmen that it seems impossible to reconcile oneself to God, let alone be a minister of

35

reconciliation to others.

A common saying that still applies to businessmen and professionals is: "The cobbler's son never has any shoes."

Once when I was speaking to a church group about the importance of having a will, my wife raised her hand and asked, "John, does that go for lawyers, too?" I hadn't been following my own advice.

It seems there is always something more that has to be done—whether it's trying a new business venture or perfecting a product or going out for a business engagement during the evening or simply staying late at the office to catch up on some paperwork.

But my main problem wasn't the "cares of life." My main problem remained insecurity. I took more cases than I should have because I feared future cases might not come.

The result was that I was over-extended and didn't have time to serve the Lord the way I knew I should. I rationalized that the more people I met, the more people could come in contact with my Christian influence. But deep inside I knew I was wrong.

The fact was I took on more cases to make more money. I didn't trust God enough to meet my needs. I relied on my own training and expertise to keep my law practice successful. No matter how much we have, it seems, we never have quite enough. We continue running on the success-money treadmill until we finally face death—without a single friend.

I was so busy with my cases that I often didn't have time to minister to people close by who needed my help. I sincerely wanted to help and *could* help, but I simply didn't have the time. I knew other attorneys who were having marriage problems or simply need-ed a Christian friend. But I couldn't be that friend;

I was too busy.

I was also too busy to handle my own homelife the way I knew the Lord required. I have a beautiful wife and three children, but too many times they were at home while I was at the office late or counseling someone. When I got home, I would sincerely wonder, "How do I fit it all in?"

Yet, I was giving lip service to so much of God's calling on my life. Despite the numerous Christian activities I managed to squeeze into my busy schedule, I still followed my own goals rather than God's plan for my life.

As a result I often became mentally dull, didn't devote quality time to those I loved, and felt deeply frustrated.

It is so easy for professionals to be overloaded with work. They get caught in a rut. And the only difference between a rut and a grave is that a grave is closed at both ends.

I was like other professionals whose end goals are more important than the present. Because I feared the future, I worked to make my future secure and ended up missing the present.

Many professionals and businessmen in our country have been told that hard work and a degree guarantee financial success. Too many of them later discover that this is a myth.

In our nation, finances and power are set goals. In the legal profession, attorneys fortunate enough to achieve financial prosperity often turn their eyes toward power—usually somewhere in politics. While some Christian attorneys work to achieve their own goals, God all the time is whispering in their ears that they should take better care of their families and heal broken relationships they have with former friends and business associates.

For myself, I was often too busy with my goals to stop and hear God.

Then God flashed some very distinct warning signs in my path.

I saw several attorneys with excellent law practices die of heart attacks. Most of them were in their forties. These men worked hard to achieve their goals only to die before they could enjoy the fruits of their labors.

I also remembered a fine young man who served as a Navy lawyer during the Vietnam War years. Shortly after his release from active duty, he discovered he had stomach cancer. Within a month he died. He left behind a wife who was expecting their first child. His death haunted me and was a constant reminder that there was no guarantee I would ever achieve my personal goals.

These deaths made me re-examine my own life and motives as a Christian attorney.

One day I read Matthew 16:25-26, and the verses jumped out at me: "For whosoever will save his life shall lose it: and whosoever will lose his life for my sake shall find it. For what is a man profited, if he shall gain the whole world, and lose his own soul? or what shall a man give in exchange for his soul?"

I knew this verse applied to non-Christians who relied on their own acumen rather than on God's leading. These were people who tried to make their own way in life, who wanted recognition from their peers and the world instead of seeking God. And some of them who achieved or were on the threshold of great worldly gain died.

Certainly I wasn't like them, was I? "That verse applies to non-Christians," I told myself.

But in my heart I knew differently. My Christian

life was often just as out of balance as their lives were.

I knew God was calling me to a deeper commitment —to be a minister of reconciliation as an attorney. I discovered that the times I trusted Him, He dramatically healed marriages that to the natural mind were hopelessly broken.

I had also witnessed parents and children reconciled to each other. Where hate, bitterness, and rejection had reigned, Christ's love covered the multitude of sins and brought families back together.

I wanted to be a 24-hour-a-day Christian attorney. I didn't want to compartmentalize my religion. I had seen many attorneys who kept their Christianity for Sunday and their law practice for the rest of the week. They hadn't integrated their Christian walk into every area of their lives.

As a result, they rationalized some of their ethical practices. They fought like the devil for their clients while acting like a saint in church.

As my Christian law practice continued to grow, I knew I had to abandon my own way of doing things. Until I surrendered my practice totally to Him, I wouldn't be the vessel He needed.

When I followed my own goals, I was subject to failure—as I discovered when I handled a major medical malpractice suit.

Had I not been so intent on following my own goals, I would have been more spiritually alert. On the surface the case looked good for the plaintiff who came to my office to seek my assistance. He claimed that a cardiologist had injured him during a heart catheterization. He said he had lost partial use of one of his legs as a result.

From the facts it appeared there was negligence on the part of the physician and the hospital, but often the facts in difficult cases unfold slowly through discovery and extensive investigation.

I agreed to represent the man and then discovered that the doctor, against whom we filed suit, was one of the most widely respected cardiologists in the Southeast.

And shortly after that I also discovered he was a Christian. I was aware of the apostle Paul's strong words to the Corinthian church in 1 Corinthians 6:1-11. He had told them in very plain terms that they were not to take a brother to court!

By accepting the case, I was forced to violate the Word. I knew I was in trouble. I had to go against the very things the Lord had been teaching me as a Christian attorney.

The case lingered on for almost three years. And all during that time I was constantly reminded that I was taking a brother to court.

When the case finally came to trial, it lasted only two days. Because the doctor was so widely respected, I couldn't get an expert witness to testify against him.

The judge, who later became a member of the Florida Supreme Court, decided we did not have sufficient evidence to let the case go the jury, and he directed a verdict for the cardiologist and the hospital.

I was humiliated. I was not accustomed to losing cases—especially in such an embarrassing way. We hadn't even gotten the case before a jury.

After the trial I went up to the doctor and congratulated him and his attorney. This is the polite word and handshake that trial attorneys with professional "class" are supposed to give—whether they feel like it or not.

I told the doctor I had not known that he was a

Christian when I took the case. Then I offered my apologies. He accepted them.

But in my heart I knew I had to do more than give a simple professional exchange.

About eight months later I spoke to a "coffee-hour" gathering at a church. Among those present was the doctor. Again I was reminded that I had taken a brother to court. After the meeting I went up to him to make sure there were no hard feelings.

I went back to my office later and considered the matter ended. But God told me that I had to do more. He wanted me to go to the doctor personally and humbly ask his forgiveness.

I called the doctor's office and made an appointment to see him. When I got there, however, the doctor was not in. He had been detained in surgery and left word that he would be late. If I couldn't wait, his nurse informed me, the doctor would understand.

For an instant I weighed my options. I quickly concluded that my only action would be to wait for the doctor to return.

I sat in his office, knowing I was going to have to humble myself in a few minutes. And I knew it was because I had not been surrendering my goals to Christ the way He required.

He wanted me to trust Him. Instead, because of my insecurities, I took on too many cases without having the time to check all the facts. My blunder had cost me an important case. But it had also taught me a valuable lesson.

In a short time the doctor arrived and invited me into his office. I told him I had to ask his forgiveness for what I had done.

I had apologized before but had never seriously asked forgiveness from my Christian brother.

He understood and forgave me. We were reconciled to each other. The ordeal had been long and painful for me, but God had taught me a lasting lesson about goals as well as about reconciliation with a brother.

More than ever I realized that God wanted me to trust Him totally. I could not rely on my own natural abilities to handle all the cases and human problems that came my way as an attorney.

I also knew I had to trust God with my finances completely.

While I was debating what to do, I thought of Matthew 6:33: "Seek ye first the kingdom of God, and his righteousness; and all these things shall be added unto you."

It was time to be more dependent on Him than on my own skills. I whittled down my caseload, trusting God to supply my financial needs.

I even resigned my position in a law firm in 1980 and maintained an independent law practice so that if I failed, I would not be a financial detriment to the firm or to anyone else.

With fewer cases, I could be home at a reasonable hour after work. I began practicing reconciliation in my family. I had seen too many professionals follow their own goals, only to have their families fall apart.

I knew that a Christian attorney with a bad marriage was not a witness for Christ despite his actions in the courtroom and with clients. His own life betrayed him.

I took my son and some other boys on a ten-day wilderness camping trip in July of 1982. Previously, my idea of "camping out" was a Holiday Inn—and the boys quickly realized I was a tenderfoot. The experiences we shared created a strong bond for a lifelong friendship with my son Randy.

Reconciling myself to my family built unity and trust. It felt so good to come home to an atmosphere of love. This was one of the rewards of putting God's will first.

I also vowed never again to become an over-extended Christian. I had been an over-extended lawyer; I could just as easily over-extend in "Christian service"—church committees, Sunday school teacher, social service organizations, *ad infinitum.* I couldn't do everything just because there was a need!

Balance became the watchword in my total life.

With fewer cases I could devote more quality time to each case, with gratifying results. My practice became a greater witness to other lawyers.

As my life and law practice became more balanced, I noticed another benefit. My mind was sharper.

I think some lawyers feel that surrendering their lives completely to Jesus means they will have to give up their intellect. However, God wants all of us— body, spirit, and soul (the intellect and emotions).

Not only does God use every bit of intelligence we possess; He also supplies us with wisdom from above. James 1:5 tells us that if we lack wisdom (which I certainly did), we can ask God who will give it generously to us.

I would like to announce that as soon as I stepped out in faith, God took over and gave me the greatest financial blessing of my entire law career. This wasn't the case. The first year I made about the same as I had for several previous years. I had no large settlements to brag about, and it probably was just as well.

If God had prospered me even more than He had done in the past, I might have turned serving Jesus into my own financial racket. I didn't surrender my law practice to Jesus in order to make a lot of money. I did it because He required it of me.

On the other hand, I didn't take a vow of poverty either. Matthew 6:33 says, "And all these things shall be added unto you." I believed the Word. During that first year when I drastically cut my caseload, God met my needs. I learned about His faithfulness.

The next year He blessed me more financially than at any previous time in my law career—even though I had fewer cases.

In my law practice I often have to ask the question, "Is what I'm doing honoring John Jones, or is it honoring You, God?"

I have to continue to reconcile myself and my legal practice back to God so that it is not my work but His work. And when I do that, I can minister reconciliation to others. I can reconcile brother with brother and reconcile others back to God. I can attempt to reconcile husband back to wife and parents back to children because I have reconciled my own practice to God.

We have all been called to a ministry of reconciliation. We have all been called to practice God's system of justice—and that system calls for brothers to be reconciled to each other. If lawyers would view themselves as instruments of reconciliation rather than as prosecutors or defenders in an adversarial relationship, the economics of this nation could be turned around. Court dockets would be reduced because husbands and wives were not taking each other to court to get a divorce. The juvenile court system would become manageable as parents and children were reconciled to each other rather than having children commit criminal acts in order to get attention from parents who forgot how to love them or didn't have the time.

Too often today in America we have injustice for all. The victims of crime are not compensated. It may even be more expensive for a victim to get justice than it would have been to do nothing at all. But in God's system of reconciliation, everyone wins. Those who are the aggressor and those who are the victims, both are healed, and God gives forgiveness and love. I believe the highest calling a lawyer can have is a call to reconciliation. I believe the highest calling a man, woman, or child can have is a calling to reconciliation. And Christ has given us all that calling. We have to determine how we will answer.

4

Reconciled
to God's Power

In my own power I could never be a minister of reconciliation. People with crippled bodies or broken relationships need more than legal advice to become whole.

Presently, ninety percent of my law practice involves personal-injury and wrongful-death cases. People injured in motor vehicle, job-related, or other accidents come to me for help in settling their claims. They have been injured by the fault, neglect, or irresponsibility of another person or business. But many of them need more than a claims settlement. They need Christ to heal their lives.

When they come to me for help, I often have the privilege of praying for their healing. This seems rather foolish to many lawyers. If God heals my client, he won't have a claim against anybody, and I will not make any money.

Some lawyers even feel that praying for clients is a breach of ethical standards between the lawyer and the client. After all, the lawyer should try to help the client receive the maximum settlement or judgment due him and leave the praying to the professionals—preachers, priests, and rabbis.

I personally believe there is no amount of money that can adequately compensate a person who has been seriously injured. For example, how much money should be awarded a young person who has been totally paralyzed for the rest of his life as a result of an accident that was not his fault?

Money is simply the only measure our society has to try to compensate an injured person. The plan was first instituted by Moses in the Old Testament to make proper restitution and prevent civil unrest and anarchy among the people.

But money is not the answer to all problems. If God heals an injured person, he can resume a normal life and not have to suffer with a permanent handicap.

I know of many Christian doctors who pray for their patients at the same time they are medically assisting them. I feel it is just as important for a Christian lawyer to pray for his clients—not only for medical healing but for the resolution of their specific legal problems. This does not diminish the need for the highest and best professional competence; this is simply looking at a total resolution of the person's problem rather than just a legal solution. An attorney is supposed to be a problem solver, not a problem causer. Often the public does not see lawyers this way. It is time for lawyers to evaluate our profession and actions. We should be part of the solution—not the cause of people's problems.

One day I received a telephone call from a man who

had been in a serious automobile-motorcycle accident. He was physically unable to come to the office and asked if I could visit him at home.

When I met Bob, he looked like a mummy in a swinging trapeze. He had more plaster and tape than a drywall company. It was hard to figure out where the sheets ended and Bob began. Bob worked at an electronics firm, and while riding his motorcycle home from work, he had been hit broadside by a car that ran a stop sign.

Bob suffered multiple fractures of the leg, the arm, and the collarbone, among numerous other injuries. More than a month later he was still at home in traction, slowly recovering from the accident.

After much painful treatment and therapy, Bob had reached the maximum medical improvement that doctors thought possible. Bob's orthopedic surgeon stated that Bob had a twenty-percent permanent impairment of the body as a whole and believed he would never again be able to perform certain body movements.

The medical evidence confirmed the bleak diagnosis. X-rays and other medical tests revealed severe alignment problems with the bones that had to mend. One medical test revealed a permanent shortage of the leg. A doctor's medical report stated that Bob would never be able to raise his arms completely above his head and that he had a thirty- to fifty-percent limitation in range of motion of the upper body. He was in a real mess.

Bob was a Christian and needed help. He wanted to once again be normal. As I listened to his story, I knew we should agree in prayer for his complete recovery. The doctors had said he was always going to have a limp and that he never would be able to raise his arms over his head.

Before Bob and I ended our conversation, we bowed our heads and prayed that he would fully recover from his injuries—despite the conclusive medical evidence.

I helped Bob on his case, and after the insurance companies thoroughly investigated the situation and examined Bob with their own doctors, they awarded him a substantial settlement.

They did not consider that God is above medical reports and facts. Over a period of time, as Bob and I continued to pray for his complete recovery, he noticed some dramatic changes. The leg, arm, and collarbone which x-rays revealed had been permanently damaged were completely mended. Bob did not limp! The arms which medical tests showed could never be raised above Bob's head now moved freely!

Bob's healing reinforced my conviction that God is interested in every aspect of our lives and total resolution of our problems. God wants to heal the entire person.

When we are reconciled to His power in every area of our lives, He will do more through us than we ever imagined possible.

However, letting the power of the Spirit touch others' lives had often been difficult for me in my earlier Christian walk. (And Old Sluefoot is still around to warn me about all the problems of ministering in a professional setting—like fear of failure, losing clients, and lack of peer acceptance.)

Two years after I had made a serious commitment of my life to Christ in 1969, an Air Force pilot talked to me about the "baptism in the Holy Spirit" and the power it brought to believers' lives.

What he said was new to me, and as a lawyer I wanted to make certain this "baptism" was valid. I had attended church on a regular basis from childhood through college and never heard about this experience. I thought I must have missed the Sunday the pastor taught on the subject. I am thankful I approached this spiritual truth without childhood bias or prejudice—simply an inquiring mind. I researched the subject as I would a legal problem.

I studied the Bible for weeks. I read Christ's promise in John 14-16 that the Father would send the Holy Spirit to be in believers. I examined the book of Acts to see what the Holy Spirit did in people's lives after He had baptized them in the Holy Spirit on the Day of Pentecost.

"Could this baptism possibly be for today?" I wondered. My answer came quickly.

One evening my wife was baptized in the Holy Spirit. She was alone in prayer when she had this experience—no peer pressure or sensationalism, simply a genuine move of God keeping His promise to one of His children. Now I had a flesh-and-blood specimen to observe.

I noticed a definite change in Carolyn's life, although I was very skeptical—most lawyers are. Her love became even more tender toward me and others. She became more sensitive to people's needs and prayed as though she believed God was going to answer her prayers. She had power in her life that I still lacked.

After thorough investigation and personal struggle, I concluded that the baptism in the Holy Spirit is for today. I had finished the research. Now it was time to try it and see the results.

One evening Carolyn and I went for dessert to the man's home who had first talked to us about the baptism in the Holy Spirit. We all prayed together, and I asked God to give me the same thing that the Church received on the Day of Pentecost.

Evidently God knew that even lawyers need extra power to overcome the world, the flesh, and the devil. I was baptized in the Holy Spirit—the verdict was in.

Immediately, I had a new sense of Christ's reality and presence; I received a prayer language that was given by the Holy Spirit. When I didn't know how to pray for needs and problems, the Holy Spirit, in His language, prayed through me much as the apostle Paul had described in Romans 8:26-27:

> Likewise the Spirit also helpeth our infirmities: For we know not what we should pray for as we ought; but the Spirit itself maketh intercession for us with groanings which cannot be uttered.
>
> And he that searcheth the hearts knoweth what is the mind of the Spirit, because he maketh intercession for the saints according to the will of God.

The baptism in the Holy Spirit also gave me a greater hunger for the Word and for Truth. And I desired more than ever to line up my life, including my business, with God's principles.

I had tapped into a power source beyond my intellect and understanding.

But I had much to learn about letting God's power flow through my life smoothly and effectively. I lived in the real world with all its problems, and I had to learn how to use this new resource. The problems were still there; however, I had a new approach to them. I would commit them to God first and seek His guidance as I used my ability to solve them. Proverbs 3:5-6 took on new meaning in my life: "Trust in the Lord with all thine heart; and lean not unto thine own understanding. In all thy ways acknowledge him and he shall direct thy paths."

This was different from my former approach of "If all else fails, try God."

After I was baptized in the Holy Spirit, I thought someone had tampered with my Bible. Many portions of the Word came alive to me. I believed them and claimed them as my own—especially verses on divine healing.

Isaiah 53:5 said, "With his stripes we were healed," and I applied that verse to my life. I knew Christians could walk in divine health. We were no longer bound to the curse of sickness.

"If any man be in Christ, he is a new creature: old things are passed away; behold, all things are become new," 2 Corinthians 5:17 said, and this verse applied to my health now that I was following the Lord.

One day I went to the office and told my law partners that we were going to drop our group health insurance policies. "Christians don't have to be sick," I said. "Christ wants us to walk in divine health."

They looked at me as though I had already lost my mental health. "Christ hasn't removed death," they argued. "You may be a Christian, but you're still going to die. And what about all the people in the hospitals?" they asked. After a few minutes, I realized that the other lawyers did not share my excitement and enthusiasm for this new spiritual truth. Neither did their wives or our staff.

But my arguments and position in the law firm caused a change in our office policy. I obviously had taken the minority position on this point and received exactly one vote for my position. I dropped the coverage, and they purchased their own policies.

My family stayed healthy, and I praised God for His

divine provisions for His children. I couldn't understand why other people didn't walk in the same revelation I had. They were missing so much.

One evening our family was invited over to our church administrator's house for dinner. He also invited a visiting minister and his family to spend the evening.

As we sat around the dinner table, I shared how my family was walking in divine health. I excitedly told them my two-year-old son had never been ill. "And since Carolyn and I discovered divine health in the Word, we haven't been sick either," I boasted.

I reminded the dinner guests of Isaiah 53:5, James 5:16-18, and other verses to show them that divine health could be theirs also.

Near the end of my spiritual message, two-year-old Randy walked into the dining room. "Mommy, I think I'm sick," he muttered. And with that he promptly deposited his stomach's belongings onto the dining room carpet.

I was chagrined. I couldn't deny the fact that my son was ill although I confessed divine health. And I was forced to eat humble pie right in front of the church administrator and a minister.

Through that incident God got a message to my heart: "Son, I'm not your servant; you're My servant."

I knew God still loved me—He hadn't surrendered me to Satan's power. I felt His love continue to surround me.

I learned a big lesson. I was to walk in all of the truth, not in partial truth. And I had much more to learn.

I had a tendency to believe in instantaneous answers. When I prayed, I expected instant results.

Perhaps I couldn't walk in perfect health, but certainly if I became ill, God would hear my prayer and immediately restore me.

My spiritual theories were soon put to the test.

One day I was at the office and felt ill. It didn't take me long to realize I was coming down with the flu. I quickly prayed for God's healing—but continued to get worse.

I went home and felt miserable. Not only was I sicker than I could ever remember, but I was going to miss a big football weekend at Florida State University in Tallahassee.

I was so ill I couldn't even walk to the bathroom. I crawled on all fours and prayed as I crawled. I quoted verses of Scripture on healing although I was in agony. "Why doesn't God heal me?" I wondered.

I finally made it to the bathroom, and suddenly God spoke to my heart, "If I've healed you, why are you down there on the floor? Get off the floor."

I got off the floor, and my strength returned. "God's healed me. I'm well," I told Carolyn. "Let's go to Tallahassee for the weekend."

Carolyn questioned whether I was really healed or whether I was simply confessing I was because of my love for football and the "Seminoles." But we quickly packed the car and headed to Tallahassee, planning to stay the weekend in a nice motel.

We stayed overnight, and the next morning when Carolyn awoke, she was terribly ill.

I knew just what to do. I pulled out the Bible, got some oil, and sat down on her bed.

I said to Carolyn, " 'By His stripes we were healed.' I'm going to anoint you with oil as James 5:14 instructs, and we're going to pray."

God had healed me; I was confident He was going to

touch my wife. We bowed our heads and earnestly asked God to take away Carolyn's terrible flu. Then I waited for God to move.

And I waited.

Nothing happened. Carolyn's flu remained. All weekend she was relegated to the motel room bed, sipping chicken soup.

Through this experience I began to understand more of God's ways. He is sovereign. He doesn't work through our formulas, I discovered. He works to fulfill His good pleasure.

Again I saw God wasn't my valet. He was a loving Father who wanted to train me up in the way that I should go so that as I matured, I would stay on His path.

And God was faithful to continue my training. At the time, I was teaching a Sunday school class, and we discussed healing. Whenever I read something to the class, I had to put on my glasses. Those extra lenses seemed to be mocking my belief in a God of miracles.

I knew God could heal my eyes, and I felt in my heart that God *was* going to heal them. I told my Sunday school class what I felt. "You watch," I said, "God is going to heal my eyesight."

They watched.

Week after week I stood before them, glasses firmly in place. "God's going to heal my eyes," I kept telling them.

Months passed. Every time I took off my glasses, things were blurred.

I continued to pray and believe God, and my Sunday school class continued to watch their bespectacled instructor.

One day I went to have my Florida driver's license renewed. My license indicated I had to wear glasses while driving. "Just for the fun of it," the licensing examiner said, "why don't you see what you can read without your glasses."

I took off my glasses and began reading, first with one eye and then with the other. I rattled off the letters as the examiner directed me to read line by line in the optical device.

"You've got twenty/twenty vision in both eyes," he said. "I'm going to remove the restriction from your driver's license."

God had healed me.

A few days later I related this story to an optometrist who was a client. He was doubtful and said these examiners often made mistakes and he wanted medical verification. He examined me the next day, and, sure enough, my eyes were normal.

And I began to understand how God does things in His timing.

My Sunday school class rejoiced with me over God's healing power. God was concerned with my health and welfare. He did care for me. I saw more than ever that God wanted me to be natural with Him in all areas of my life. I wasn't to use Him. I was to surrender to Him. And He would give me all the things that a loving Father has for His children.

God didn't want me to play games with Him. He wanted me to be honest. When I turned my problems over to Him, He took them. I couldn't heal my own eyes, but He could.

And I didn't know all the right things to do. My formulas didn't work. My religious words didn't change things. But when I honestly came to Him, recognizing His sovereignty and allowing Him to have His way, He did things beyond what my natural thinking could ever imagine.

All during my years of surrendering my practice to God, He continued to give me tangible evidence that He was working in my law practice, helping me with cases and bringing about miraculous results whenever I trusted Him.

One such case involved Chad. He was charged with embezzling money from a company. It was a criminal felony case held before a circuit judge who, at the time, had a reputation as one of the toughest criminal judges in the area. The newspapers loved to follow his trials because of his reputation and dramatic flair. Chad faced a possible five-year sentence in state prison.

Just before the Christmas holidays I came to the courthouse for the "sounding of the docket for the trial week." As a trial attorney, I wanted to confirm the exact time the case was to be tried. I expected the case to be handled after the first of the year, but when I talked to the judge, he surprisingly said, "You're picking the jury in an hour the next floor down." The nine cases ahead of our case had been continued or changed pleas at the last minute, and it was court time for Chad and me. What a wonderful way to start a week, especially the week before Christmas!

The trial lasted two days. And after the jury went to make their deliberations, the judge told me, "If your client gets convicted, he's going to spend Christmas in jail. He's going directly from this courtroom to the jail.

"Besides that," he said, "I've heard all the testimony, and I believe he's guilty. I'm going to give you one last chance to enter a plea, and I'll withhold adjudication of guilt and let him go home for the holidays, while pre-sentence investigation is being completed. If he has no prior criminal record, I'll give him probation."

He continued, "I want to go to a Christmas party, the prosecutor wants to go to a Christmas party, and you are still insistent on your client's innocence."

I returned to Chad and repeated the judge's comments. "I believe I'm innocent," Chad told me, "and I trust my fate to the Lord on whether I go to jail or whether I go home." Chad and I got down on our knees in the deserted courtroom to pray for God's intervention.

After we prayed, I returned and told the judge of our decision. The judge's comment was, "He is *wrong!* He is going away."

"My client and I are trusting God," I responded, "and we want to hear the jury's verdict."

Several hours later the jury returned with the verdict: "Innocent!" We had trusted God, and His power was a witness to all of us—including the judge.

In my own life and law practice I didn't want to be a hindrance to God or to others. I had other lessons to learn about being equipped as a minister of reconciliation. I was still in the construction process: God was not through with me yet.

5

Sloppy Agape

One of the first things I discovered after accepting Christ into my life is the different types of love. From the past I understood *eros* (romantic love) and *phileo* (love for family and friends), but now I had the chance to walk in something new and exciting—*agape*.

Christ's own actions were the manifestation of agape. His was a tough love that withstood crucifixion on Good Friday. His was a compassionate love that made Him deny himself in order to save those He loved. His was a love that would reconcile the world back to the Father.

And I wanted to extend the same agape to everyone I met. What I ended up extending all too often, however, was a compromise—sloppy agape.

One of my first memorable encounters with sloppy agape happened when I was looking for a secretary for my fledgling law practice.

I asked several Christian business friends if they knew of anyone who would be able to help me.

"I know just the person for you, John," one Christian businessman immediately responded. "She works in my office and is a fine Christian woman. She is looking for a job with more future and challenge."

My friend told me more about her, and what he said sounded like an answer to prayer.

I superficially interviewed the woman and offered her a position with my firm. She accepted, and I thought my secretarial problems were over.

But shortly after she came to work for me, my bubble burst. The new secretary couldn't seem to concentrate on the job; her mind was on other things, and she had no legal secretarial experience. She didn't really have the skills that my Christian business friend said she had. Instead of helping my law practice, she actually became a hindrance.

Something was definitely wrong, and I decided to do some personal investigation to solve the problem. After asking several people some very pointed questions, I learned the truth.

The Christian businessman who gave my new secretary such a glowing recommendation was, I discovered, under orders to find a new, respectable job for the secretary.

I also learned that these orders had come to my friend from the company president's wife, who thought the personal relationship between her husband and the secretary was interfering with the business operation.

My Christian business friend had never told me this. Instead, he used me to solve his own problem. I had been duped by a person who hadn't given me "full disclosure." I had been told half-truths, and because he was a Christian, I took them at face value.

But the fault was as much mine as his. I hadn't used discernment when I hired the secretary. Also, I had acted on emotion instead of looking at all the facts. Placing emotion above spiritual discernment is, I quickly learned, one of the chief traits of sloppy agape.

My law partner finally bailed me out of my problem. He confronted the secretary and explained why she wasn't working out in our law firm. Then he terminated her.

At the time, I didn't agree with my partner's actions. I thought he was harsh. How could a Christian fire another Christian?

Later I knew he was correct. She had been hired under false pretenses and did not have her personal life in order. Also, she was quickly becoming frustrated with the work in the law firm because it was beyond her ability.

My partner had taken a hard but necessary step. If he and I were to be good, efficient attorneys, we needed those around us who understood our goals and who would help us. We needed those whose lives were in balance so that their problems wouldn't carry over into our law practice.

But I was a slow learner when it came to hiring people. I continued to hire people on the basis of emotion. If Christians were in trouble and needed a job, I looked for ways to hire them. It didn't matter that the person couldn't type or knew nothing about bookkeeping. I reacted out of emotion rather than wisdom.

James 1:5, says, "If any man lack wisdom, let him ask of God, that giveth to all men liberally, and upbraideth not; and it shall be given him."

I was too busy trying to meet every need I saw to be able to seek wisdom. The other lawyers finally told me that I shouldn't hire people; I was too emotional in the decisions.

Some of those I hired were emotional cripples, recovering from a divorce or a family tragedy. I took them in, trying to solve their problems. I ended up adding to the problem when the job didn't work out for them. Not only was their self-esteem lowered; they became resentful because a Christian had rejected them.

I would have been wiser directing them to Christian counseling and helping them get the proper training so they could secure a better job in the future. Instead, I acted in sloppy agape, hurting them and frustrating myself and my law partners.

Christians feel sorry for other Christians and sometimes let their emotions get in the way of true spiritual help.

I know of one Christian woman who conducted home parties to sell a reputable product. There was nothing wrong with her product, but there was something wrong with her motives.

She held home parties for her Christian friends in order to earn additional income for the family. This also served as an escape from her home problems and lack of communication with her husband. Many of the Christian women knew of her problems and came to the home-care parties because they felt sorry for her.

If discerning Christians would have counseled her instead of accepting invitations to her home parties, her marriage and home problems could have been reconciled.

People who walk in sloppy agape don't address issues and will never be able to be effective ministers of reconciliation. They could never say, "Mary, your home is out of order" or "I believe you are using Christians for your own personal gain."

Sloppy agape overlooks sins. Instead of talking to a young man about his sex problems or to a husband about his laziness, we continue to ignore their sins and heap on more sloppy agape.

On the inside, many of these people with sin problems want someone to lead them out of their struggles. But sloppy agape Christians are afraid to discuss sin problems because they might offend a Christian brother or be rejected.

I have known criminals who wanted to be caught so that they would no longer have to carry around the weight of guilt for their actions. There are many hurting Christians, too, who want someone to lead them into wholeness.

Sloppy agape does not have the power to deal with problems when they arise. Instead of talking to a couple who are having a marriage problem in the church, sloppy agape Christians pretend the problem doesn't exist. They "love" the troubled couple when they're around them and talk about their problem when they're not around.

The troubled couple interprets the sloppy agape actions as *de facto* acceptance of what they're doing. The marriage problems are never confronted in the wisdom of the Spirit, and Satan wins another victory by default in the marriage war.

For years I was afraid to be totally honest with those in trouble. I put my arms around them and said, "I love you."

"Thanks, John. I needed that," they responded.

But their problems didn't go away. They needed more than emotional comfort. They needed tough agape to break into their lives and heal their hurts.

There is such a need in the world for Christians who minister with spiritual discernment. They will dare to confront sin, knowing that Christ has overcome the world—including the sin problems that many Christians still have.

Our sloppy agape even extends to God. If we only throw out one-line prayers to God while we cruise down the freeway to get to work, we know God will understand. After all, I have to feed my family; God requires that of me. He will understand if I only have time for a quick prayer as I drive to work. After working all day, we are too tired to pray at home; again we rationalize God will understand.

Our sloppy agape releases us from accountability with God. Christ died for us; He forgives our sins. If I make a mistake, He is right there to forgive me. But in all our rationalizations we forget God's admonition in 1 Peter 1:16, "Be ye holy; for I am holy."

To walk in Christ's agape takes sacrifice. It means speaking loving truth when it might be rejected. It means sacrificing time to lead others into wholeness. It means being willing to be used of God instead of using God.

Some Christian parents are not willing to put forth the self-sacrifice that agape requires at home. Parents have to die to themselves; they must give up some of their own freedom and pleasures so that they can spend enough time with the children to really nurture them in the Lord. It becomes much easier to give a sacrifice of money or toys than to give a sacrifice of one's own time to the children.

It may be easier to give a child a toy than to teach him how to fish. Learning to fish requires time and energy; it requires sacrifice. It may take quite a bit of agape on the parent's part. But then the parent is giving the child something that will last him a lifetime.

All the animal sacrifices in the Old Testament demonstrate that substitutes could not replace the real thing. The human race needed the sacrifice of the Lamb of God to take away the sin of the world. Christian parents are discovering that the same rule applies to them. Cheaply bought sheep are not a permanent substitute. To save a child, the parent is going to have to make a personal sacrifice.

A Christian walking in sloppy agape is out of balance. And his view of the Word is often off-center also. He sometimes removes verses from their scriptural context and applies them to situations he encounters. He expects a miraculous cure-all because he has quoted the verses of Scripture. John 15:7 says, "If ye abide in me, and my words abide in you, ye shall ask what ye will, and it shall be done unto you." But often sloppy agape doesn't make time to abide in Christ. Instead, God is selfishly used as a servant to meet our needs.

A spiritually sensitive Christian will be willing to satisfy God's desire first. God seeks a people to worship and love Him.

Hebrews 5:14 describes mature Christians as those who "by reason of use have their senses exercised to discern both good and evil." Many in the body of Christ have to give up their sloppy agape and start developing discernment.

Unscrupulous people are very eager to take advantage of Christians who exist by sloppy agape. Many organizations and businesses know that church people want to help others. They give their money more freely than others in our society and are more trusting.

So some marketing organizations gear their products toward gullible Christians. They ask Christians to invest in their worthy cause or their "Christian" product, knowing the Christian mentality.

I have even observed Christian businessmen taking advantage of these same Christians. The businessmen have their own love priorities totally reversed.

First Timothy 6:10 describes their problem: "For the love of money is the root of all evil: which while some coveted after, they have erred from the faith, and pierced themselves through with many sorrows."

As a lawyer my ears have been opened to many complaints about Christians using other Christians for personal gain. People who practice sloppy agape often fall prey to those who wear their Christianity externally. True agape is more than wearing Christian lapel pins. Discerning Christians must look to the heart of things to protect themselves and others from being abused.

I have heard people lament that they lost large investments because they trusted entrepreneurs who professed to be Christians. If the entrepreneur is really a Christian, he shouldn't mind having others investigate his stock deal or land investment claim. He would have nothing to hide.

New Christians who happen to have money are quick victims for pseudo-Christian con men. People using Christian phrases get them to invest in land schemes or some kind of "Christian" ministry, and soon the new Christian is fleeced. A strong, discerning Church will protect its babes from "Christian" scams.

Christian businessmen who walk in sloppy agape are often victims of their own weaknesses. They are afraid to confront someone else in honesty—afraid they will be misunderstood.

As a Christian lawyer I have often been called by Christians who want to "take advantage" of my services. Many of these people expect my services for little or no cost because we are both Christians. They never give me the chance to bless them with a gift of my services when the Holy Spirit directs. Instead, they come to me only to get something for nothing.

I have had to be wary of Christians who told me the Lord told them to call. Then they asked me for assistance—gratis, of course. Many people know how to say all the right Christian cliches, know how to praise the Lord, and even know how to testify; but these outer signs don't mean they are sincere or that the Lord sent them.

Many Christian businessmen find themselves in a real trap because so many other Christians come to them, simply looking for a price cut or a special favor. Instead of paying a fair and honest price for the Christian businessman's services, these other Christians are actually milking their brothers in the Lord.

Many Christian businessmen have told me they can't afford any more Christian clients. They would rather have non-Christian clients because those clients follow a legitimate standard of business ethics.

In my legal practice over the years I have donated my services many times to Christians who needed my help, and I will continue to help others in the future. But I have learned that not everyone who calls himself a Christian follows Christ's standards of "fervent charity."

For years I represented people simply because they said they were Christians. Because I did not want to be a "stumbling block" to a weaker brother, I took their case or even helped them in areas of law where a different lawyer would be more knowledgeable.

I also noticed that I developed resentment toward those Christians who were taking advantage of me, their Christian brother.

Many times I was already over-extended. My family needed me at home; my caseload required my diligent attention. But my sloppy agape made me help even more people. I did not have enough courage to say no. As a result I hurt myself, my family, and sometimes the very ones I was trying to help.

Sincere Christians everywhere are afraid to say no when a need is presented. No matter how much time it takes or how much it costs them, they help anyone who asks them (and sometimes those who don't even ask them). They are like the man who was in quicksand up to his waist and calling out for someone to throw him another brick.

These Christians are afraid to offend someone else—and end up hurting themselves. They pick up their brothers' crosses and try to carry them, not realizing that their brothers have to carry their own crosses in order to mature in the Lord.

Agape is a mature love. I have seen Christians say they are speaking the truth in love and then promptly destroy another Christian whose heart was not yet ready to receive what was being said. Blunt words can have very sharp edges. We must continually examine our motives as we minister to be sure we are compelled by Christ's love and forgiveness.

We must listen to God's Spirit and follow His leading to accomplish God's will. If we don't listen, we end up frustrated.

I experienced that frustration not long ago when I made an exception to my vow with God to not handle any more domestic cases.

God's Word says in Psalm 89:34, "My covenant I have not violated, nor will I alter the utterance of my lips." I should have known that I shouldn't break my covenant with Him either.

But my emotions got in the way.

A minister referred a young man to me who had recently accepted Jesus into his life. He thought I could give him spiritual counsel.

Our Bible study group took Brad under their wing and helped him. We got him settled and found him a job.

But he still had a major problem. His wife Ginny had filed for a divorce. I felt sorry for this young Christian and offered to represent him. Certainly God wouldn't mind this exception to my vow—I was helping a new Christian, after all.

After I accepted the case, I was confronted with a tangled marriage mess. Ginny was a Christian who had been married previously. She was divorcing Brad to fulfill her marriage vows to her first husband who had also become a Christian.

She had left her first husband out of discouragement because he wouldn't become a Christian and because of other marital misunderstandings.

Brad, who had been married twice previously, came to Ginny's rescue. He was handsome and kind and invited her to stay with him. She accepted.

She was a regular church member who got caught in a trap. She tried to escape by divorcing her first husband and marrying Brad.

She and Brad moved away from the area. But things began to turn sour. Ginny realized that she had made a great mistake by leaving her first husband. She had moved in with Brad during a period of great emotional stress, and now she began to regret her actions.

She believed God wanted to restore her first marriage despite the fact she was now pregnant with Brad's child.

Ginny left Brad and went back to her first husband who by this time also desired to be reconciled.

Into this marriage maze rode John Jones, the white knight and domestic attorney. I was going to unscramble the eggs.

I quickly became emotionally involved with both Brad and Ginny. By now Ginny had turned completely against Brad, and Brad was torn apart because Ginny was pregnant with the child he had always wanted.

For myself, I became so wrapped up with both of them and their hurts that I could no longer represent Brad. I had lost any objectivity I should have had as his attorney and his Christian brother.

This was a marriage story that would not have a fairy-tale ending. The white knight would not prevail. No matter how things turned out, people were going to remain hurt. Lives would be permanently scarred. That was hard for me to accept.

If I had not accepted Brad's case in the first place, I might have been able to stay objective enough to help him and Ginny spiritually stabilize their lives even if Ginny returned to her first husband. As it turned out, I could help neither.

The example of Brad and Ginny is a vivid object lesson to the Church. Much of what happened in the first place could have been prevented if the Church had been mindful of its weaker members.

Ginny was alone and hurt when she had her initial problems with her first husband. She sang in the choir and attended church regularly. But when she ran into marriage difficulties, no one stepped in to counsel her. If the church had been practicing the ministry of reconciliation, she and her first husband could have been counseled. But the church didn't get involved. It couldn't hear the bleating of one of its own wounded sheep.

If someone had helped Ginny earlier, she might not have acted so hastily to leave her husband and live openly in sin with another man while she was filing for a divorce.

In my years of counseling and as an attorney I have seen so many people make great mistakes simply because they did not wait quite long enough for God to bring about the answers His way. And brothers and sisters in Christ were afraid to get involved.

By the time I got involved with Brad and Ginny, it was too late to change things back to where they had been. There was no safe or easy way out of the mess. If only I had met Brad or Ginny sooner. If only someone in the church had seen her plight and stopped her from making such destructive decisions. If only we hadn't been walking in sloppy agape.

For Ginny, for her first husband, for Brad, and for Ginny and Brad's new child it is too late to undo the mistakes. You cannot relive the past. But for many Ginnys and Brads it is still not too late if members of the body of Christ dare to get involved in others' lives and dare to be ministers of reconciliation to their hurts.

The body of Christ must tell people with weak marriages that divorce is not the answer; it is just the beginning of much greater problems.

Those who see a marriage in trouble have to do more than pray for them. They must get personally involved in their lives.

Sloppy agape won't be able to help the Brads and Ginnys all around us. Christ's powerful love is needed. And I have found that true agape flows through me to others when I walk in accountability.

6

Accountability

Shortly after I entered private law practice
in 1972, I accepted a client because he said he was a
Christian. He was a wealthy entrepreneur who had all
the right Christian phrases and cliches. He knew how
to talk the spiritual language, and he glittered when
he walked.

He wanted a Christian lawyer to work for him.

Against the advice of my wife, who said I should
stay away from him, I accepted him as a major client.
I traveled around the nation in private and commer-
cial planes and rode in a chauffeured limousine and
thought serving Jesus was pretty good.

However, as time passed, I learned the difference
between external and internal spirituality. My client
asked me to do some things that I did not consider
ethical, and I was confronted with a moral decision.
Should I follow my Christian convictions, or should I

stay with this man to protect my financial security?

Very quickly I knew I had to end my relationship with him. I learned that Christians cannot judge others by external evidence. The evidence must be spiritually discerned.

God started showing me, too, that I had to take time to be with Him and hear His voice. Christ had to escape from the crowd to spend time fellowshipping with the Father. I had to do the same in order to hear His calling for me instead of following everyone else's ideas.

I finally realized I hadn't internalized my spirituality. Instead of walking in Christian labels and slogans, I needed to know my own heart. I had to be honest before God when I was alone. Only then could I be a minister of reconciliation the way God wanted me to be.

God was calling me, as He calls others who want to be ministers of reconciliation, to be accountable for my actions. One test for that accountability is to see what you do when you are in the quiet place.

When you are all alone with no one else to see you, are you still godly? When you are in another town and the wife isn't there to watch your actions, are you still spiritual? When you enter a motel room on the business trip, do you read the Word or do you watch R-rated movies on cable TV? Cliff Dudley, a widely-known Christian author and speaker, has correctly stated, "Ninety percent of men's problems are in their pants." Men must learn to control the temptations of money and sex.

To be an effective minister of reconciliation, each Christian must first clean out his personal temple.

Many times in my own Christian walk, I looked fine externally. I did the "right" things and spoke the correct spiritual words, but inside I still didn't always face myself.

The law firm I was in became known as a "Christian" law firm. At an annual meeting of the local bar association, a satirical skit was even performed showing how we conducted our cases with prayer, placed tracts on the table in the lobby, and sold Bibles to anyone who came into our office. The skit showed us answering the phone, "Brother Carroll and Deacon Jones," and people placed on hold could listen to the background music, "Jesus Loves You."

Others recognized that we were Christians. However, sometimes I think the recognition was merely because I was wearing my Christianity on my sleeve. It can become comfortable to be known as a Christian lawyer or a Christian dentist or a Christian bricklayer or a Christian truck driver.

Once you have been labeled as a Christian businessman, people will pretty much leave you alone and let you "do your own thing." You can even get a little puffed up thinking that others respect you because you are a Christian. They ask you to pray at the banquets because no one else will pray. People want you to lead the Sunday school class because you are successful both as a Christian and a businessman.

You can say, "God, I'm living for you. See, even *they* recognize it." It is so easy to get comfortable in your external Christianity that you stop really touching and changing hearts.

To prove that you are a Christian, you can pile up plenty of evidence. You can be a Sunday school teacher. You can be a Christian businessman. You can give to the poor. You can do other acts that others can see. But unless your spiritual life has been internalized, it won't mean anything to God.

When your spirituality has been internalized, you do things the Spirit wants you to do even when others do not see your actions. When a friend or a business acquaintance enters the hospital, and God tells you to send him a card or visit him, you do it. And that small token may do more than all of your other spiritual acts over the last several years.

Since 1969 I have increasingly realized that I am to perform for the audience of Jesus and not for man. That concept is what helped me take control of my professional existence.

My performance has not been perfect either. But God knew it wouldn't be. That's why He sent His Son to live through me and all who confess Jesus as Lord.

What God wants from me is my willingness to minister reconciliation to others. When I am willing, He prepares me for better service to Him. If I had to be perfect before I tried to help others, I would never help anyone.

Philippians 2:12-13 says, "Work out your own salvation with fear and trembling. For it is God which worketh in you both to will and to do of his good pleasure."

As I internalized my spirituality, God worked in me. And, amazingly, He brought more people into my life who needed answers. Sometimes they resisted the light of Christ, but at least I knew it was God and not my own acts placing them under conviction. I didn't scare away non-Christians through an external religious show.

Sometime back a Jewish woman came to my office for advice on a divorce. She had been referred to me, and as a professional courtesy to another attorney, I agreed to help her.

We began by talking about reconciliation, and

immediately I sensed a strong reaction. She did not like my Christian views nor my Christianity. For several minutes the atmosphere was icy in the room. However, I agreed to help her despite how she felt toward me. She said, "I just wish my Jewish lawyer friend who helps run our local temple could have a few minutes with you. He would set you straight on quite a few things."

On the day of the final hearing, the Jewish woman and I were sitting in the courthouse corridor waiting to go in. Coming down the hall was the Jewish attorney she wanted me to hear.

"Here comes Mark," she said. "He'll straighten you out."

I didn't tell her we were friends.

Mark came up to me, stopped, and said, "John, I'm going in for surgery tomorrow, and I would appreciate it if you would pray for me. I know you are a man of prayer and that your prayers are answered."

God had brought him there at that time to be a witness to the Jewish lady. I had not tried to force myself or my beliefs on her. She had been reacting to the light of Christ, and God brought another Jew to bear witness to that light. She saw that a Christian lawyer and Jewish lawyer could walk in reconciliation and not in animosity, and it had an effect on her attitude toward Christians.

I continue to internalize my spirituality. Sometimes, when I feel I have arrived, God shows me just where I am, and I have to fall down and ask forgiveness. None of us has arrived, but all of us can be ministers of reconciliation if we simply open our hearts to His direction, allowing Him to work on our hearts and shape us into His image.

Because heaven sometimes seems a long time off,

we don't always realize that we are accountable to God right now. It is so easy to put things off, to plan to change instead of changing.

But unless we get beyond the Christian externals, unless we stop wearing our badges that are not much different than designer labels, unless we stop talking it and start walking it, the world won't be changed, and we won't be effective ministers of reconciliation.

It's easier to talk about Christ than to trust Christ. So often in the past it has been easier for me to do the work rather than letting Christ work through me. I'm still learning and growing. It's a daily recommitment to His power to work through me. Sometimes it's a sacrifice of my flesh so that the Spirit may be made alive.

What He requires of us is an open and willing heart so that He can be the Master and we can be the instruments. Then, we will also be His ministers.

You don't have to be a man with seven theological degrees to be a minister of reconciliation. You don't have to be a millionaire or be recognized by everyone in the world to be a minister of reconciliation. You, whoever you are, wherever you are, can be that minister. If you work in a factory, you can minister reconciliation to those around you. If you are a teacher, you can minister reconciliation. If you are a housewife, you can minister reconciliation. There is always someone who is open to receive that ministry. God has called us all to it.

The little man in Christ—the butcher, the baker, the candlestick maker—is the real superstar. Second Corinthians 5:18 says God has "given us the ministry of reconciliation!" Each person in the body of Christ is called to be that minister.

We can be those ministers as we internalize our spirituality and realize we are accountable to God.

The entire system of law is predicated on the fact that people must be accountable for their actions. And the same holds true in the spiritual world.

Criminals hate law. The righteous accept the law. "We know that the law is good, if a man use it lawfully; knowing this, that the law is not made for a righteous man, but for the lawless and disobedient . . ." (1 Tim. 1:8-9).

Some people don't want to be held accountable, however. They want their own way, even though they may hurt themselves and others. As a lawyer my job is to see that people are treated fairly. But I am not to release them from the consequences of their acts.

And the same is true as ministers of reconciliation. We are to help people, not remove them from accountability.

This point was brought home to me when I had to work with Kevin, a seventeen-year-old who had been arrested for resisting a police officer with violence, trespassing, and possession of marijuana. His parents came to my office to see if I could help him.

As a criminal attorney in the adversarial relationship, I realized I had to do everything possible for each client to prevent him from being convicted. In law school I had been taught that a person is not legally guilty until proven so beyond and to the exclusion of every reasonable doubt without violating the defendant's constitutional rights.

I counseled the parents and also talked to Kevin. I told him he needed to change his life and that he should start attending church and change his personal association with certain negative people.

Then I went to court. After a one-day trial the juvenile judge found Kevin not guilty.

The young man had a "first-aid" religious experience and thanked God and me for helping him. "Thank God I got out of this scrape," he probably thought.

Within a year I had another call from Kevin's parents. He was in trouble with the law again—charged with loitering, prowling, and disturbing the peace in a residential neighborhood.

Once more I gave him my strong, fatherly lecture. "Didn't you understand from the last time that you can't do these things anymore?" I asked him.

Despite his shallow answer, I represented him again. I looked at the case and thought I could successfully defend him.

I saw that his legal rights might have been violated and that the charges were unconstitutionally vague and lacked probable cause in his case. I filed the proper motions to dismiss the case, and the judge granted my motion and dismissed the charges.

Kevin thanked me and promised one more time that this would not be repeated. But in reality he simply had another first-aid religious experience. He had seen me succeed before a judge in one county in a metropolitan area and before a totally different type of judge in a rural area.

He knew he had a good attorney. He thought he had a savior.

I thought I had done the right thing in defending him. I had prayed for him and for his family.

About eight months later I received a phone call one afternoon from a police sergent. He informed me that he had Kevin on the other end of the line, taking advantage of the one phone call he could make while in custody. The boy I had gotten off the hook twice before was calling his savior for more salvation. He told me he had been arrested for burglary of a vehicle.

I met with him and surveyed the evidence. "What are you going to do to get me out of this?" he asked me.

"I'm not going to get you out of it," I told him. "You've gotten yourself in where no one is going to be able to get you out.

"There are witnesses who saw you commit the theft. Your fingerprints are on the evidence. They retrieved the stolen item exactly where they saw you throw it. You were never out of their sight. And by the time you got home, the police pulled up right behind you. There is no way anyone can get you off the hook this time."

During the entire time I rehearsed the situation, Kevin never really heard me. He didn't realize that I couldn't be his escape hatch one more time. He thought and believed, "There is some way he is going to get me out of this. He's a good criminal lawyer. He's done it twice before. He can do it again."

After looking at all the files and conducting a thorough investigation myself, I realized there was "no legal defense" for this criminal act.

I went to the state attorney's office to arrange for a plea bargain. The judge said, "I'm going to reserve some jail time in this case."

I really wanted to prevent my client from serving any jail time because I didn't want anyone incarcerated if I could help it. To me jails are often breeding places for more criminals. I did not feel incarceration was the solution for a twenty-year-old's problems and felt it wasn't the solution for most people's problems under its present form.

I did everything I could for Kevin. However, the judge was much wiser than I and sentenced him to ten days in jail as a condition of probation.

After Kevin and I left the courtroom and walked down the hall, he turned to me and said, "Thanks, John, you really sold me down the river. You really did me in, didn't you?"

That sad episode with the young man taught me a valuable lesson—consequences must follow behavior. But at the time, I didn't see that because I looked at my obligation from strictly an ethical, legal standpoint. I was to do the best I could for my clients, which meant getting them freed whenever possible.

But I kept forgetting that some people are not ready to be helped.

Trying to help people, I became their savior. I removed the consequences of their sins from them. I was instrumental in covering up their mistakes.

I am a lawyer who practices the ministry of reconciliation. But many people have come to me not wanting to be reconciled. Many have come to me hoping I can remove the penalty for their actions.

And in a similar way many Christians go to other Christians looking for acceptance instead of discipline.

Human nature only changes through the power of Jesus Christ and not through lawyers trying to "get people off the hook."

True reconciliation means we have to help people confront themselves, ask forgiveness, and walk in repentance. If that doesn't happen, there is no true healing.

If you cut off the consequences without having people ask forgiveness and walk in true repentance, there will be no change. Repentance means turning 180 degrees. Repentant people walk in the other direction and don't continue on their old paths.

Here I was, trying to be the young man's savior, removing the consequences from him.

Reconciliation does not mean we eliminate the consequences of sin from people's lives. It means we help them through the consequences so that they may be totally healed.

But because of our "sloppy agape" actions, we wish people didn't have to face the consequences of their acts. I have found it is harder to confront them in their sin than it is to let their actions slide by and say that we will love them no matter what.

But in order for love to be real love it must be honest.

Today in the body of Christ, we have many people walking around who have not dealt with themselves. Others in the Body have not led them to be reconciled to themselves, to God, and to others. Instead, we have tried to ignore their faults. Consequently, these people continue to repeat old patterns. And they never mature.

As a parent, I hate to see any of my children suffer. I want to make things as easy for them as possible. And at times, I haven't made them face some consequences that they should have faced. But they have to learn that in order to pass a test, they have to study. In order to do well in school, they have to be disciplined. Sometimes as a parent I would rather allow them their own freedom and not be strict with them. But I know that it will cost both them and me very much later on in life. We both will reap what we have sown.

So often adults in the body of Christ are still walking around with childhood patterns. They haven't prepared for the test. They continue to flunk the same exams because they haven't studied. They haven't put in the work necessary to allow them to graduate. And until we speak truth to those who are repeating patterns of failure, they never will change.

For example, some adults haven't prepared to get a good job. They sit back thinking work will come to them. Or they may not act responsibly as an employee and thus lose their job.

Sometimes we in the Body then rush in and say to that person, "That's O.K.; we'll employ you. We'll help you out. We'll take care of you." What the person really needs is a change of direction, not another job which will repeat his failure patterns.

What we must do in addition to ministering to people's needs is call them to accountability, helping them see themselves and the actions so that positive change occurs. This is true love in action.

The Bible directs us to help the poor and take care of those in need, and I tried to practice this with everyone I met. But I had to have courage enough to deal with people as well as with their needs.

If someone in my Sunday school class had a financial need, I reached into my pocket and helped them. If someone came to my office who needed financial assistance because they had lost a job, I was quick to give them money. If someone needed comforting because they had just had a fight with their spouse, I was quick to comfort and console.

It was harder for me to "restore" someone "in the spirit of meekness" as Galatians 6:1 says—because that meant I had to discern what their *real* needs were.

Some of these people became dependent upon me rather than God. If they had blown it, they knew they could run to Brother John. They didn't have to deal with their sin problem; all those who were "weary" and "heavy laden" could come to me and I would try to give them aid.

Instead of some of these people learning the consequences of their own disobedience, they came to me as their solution, and I helped them again and again.

A person who sins must ask forgiveness and then walk in repentance. When I came between them and the convicting power of the Holy Spirit, I actually frustrated God's plan for them to walk in wholeness.

A minister of reconciliation must deal with sin. And this is so hard for us to do. It is easier for us to "love" people and allow some of them to almost become leeches on our personal lives than it is to confront them in the power of the Spirit and talk to them directly about their sin problem. When people see and confess their sins, God is faithful and just to forgive them from all unrighteousness. As ministers of reconciliation, we must make certain we don't interfere with God's plan.

We can't go back and change the past, but we can ask forgiveness for past sins. Sometimes, we confess Joel 1:25 and believe that God "will restore the years that the locust has eaten." But restoration comes when we have changed our patterns. Otherwise, we are doomed to repeat our failures until we die.

Ministers of reconciliation bring people out of the doom of repeated failures.

To minister life takes discernment. Discernment sees the inside and not the outward show. When we have internalized our spirituality and made ourselves accountable to God, He will use us to help others make life-changing decisions so that they may walk in true freedom.

7

'What God Hath Joined Together'

Divorce is a messy, messy business. And for the victims, especially Christian victims, it can be an experience with severe aftershocks that last for years.

Our society makes divorce seem natural and easy, but what TV and other media don't portray is the human agony that almost always accompanies a divorce. We don't see how deeply a marriage dissolution cuts to the very core of a person's self-esteem.

Television and movies can't really depict how divorce shatters a child's view of love and leaves him an emotional cripple for years, if not for life.

America today is becoming a "no-fault" society. Whatever a person does is not his fault. If he drinks too much, it is not his fault. If he leaves his spouse, it is not his fault. If he hurts other people along the way, it is not his fault.

Our law system has followed this same path. We are

now going to "no-fault" insurance and "no-fault" divorce.

While the Bible says we are responsible for our actions and that we reap what we sow, society says that's too hard and unfair.

So today's law system creates giant escape clauses from responsibility. One of the main examples is the no-fault divorce. We have even changed the name to "dissolution of marriage" to make it sound nicer and more palatable. Under this system people don't have to be accountable for their actions. No longer do the parties have to explain what irresponsible acts they have committed; no longer do they have to recognize their moral obligations to their spouse.

The no-fault divorce is becoming widely accepted across America. In Florida, for example, there are now only two grounds for divorce. One of the grounds for divorce is if the spouse has been committed to a mental institution or is ruled incompetent for a period of three years. The other is that the marriage is irretrievably broken.

The Bible also had few reasons for a divorce. But its reason admitted serious moral failure—adultery or fornication.

Today's divorce laws reflect the "hardness of men's hearts." For example, under the present Florida Dissolution of Marriage statute one of the marriage partners simply has to "swear" or "affirm" that the marriage is irretrievably broken. This law is similar to the no-fault divorce laws that are sweeping the entire nation.

In Moses' day a woman was considered a piece of property. A man could declare three times that he divorced his wife in her presence and give her a writing, finalizing the divorce.

Jesus thought more of women than that. He recognized that if the "two shall be one flesh," divorce should not be easy.

In the present Florida statute the preamble states that the statute is being enacted to preserve the family. Then the statute proceeds to allow marriages to be ended almost as easily as when the men of Moses' day simply said they wanted a divorce.

The Florida legislators made a provision for counseling if minor children were involved, but they didn't say who was to determine the counseling. Consequently, if the husband and wife can't or won't agree on a counselor, effective counseling usually doesn't occur. Also, most judges don't believe marital counseling will work, so they don't order it.

And, most likely, the lawyers offer little constructive counseling to their clients. If the clients reconciled, some lawyers would lose much of their financial base.

One day a Christian woman who had been married for over seventeen years came to me, seeking legal counsel.

The husband, who was a nominal Christian, had a responsible job with a national company, traveling extensively. In his times away from home he had been unfaithful to his wife.

She didn't know what to do, especially since they had three children—the oldest child, seventeen, and the youngest, nine.

I could have given her quick counsel to get a divorce. Matthew 5:32 indicates that divorce is justified if the spouse commits adultery.

But I recalled what Christ had said to the Pharisees in Mark 10:5-9 when they wanted to know if Moses' rules on divorce still applied: "But for the hardness of your hearts Moses allowed divorce. However, this was not God's first choice. From the beginning of the creation God made them male and female. For this cause shall a man leave his father and mother, and cleave to his wife; and the two shall be one flesh; so then they are no more two, but one flesh. What therefore God hath joined together, let no man put asunder" (paraphrased).

I told her frankly that she had legal and scriptural grounds for divorce but that I also believed God could reconcile her marriage. Before our session ended, I gave her a copy of the book, *Second Chance*. This book, written by David Van Wade and his wife Sarah, honestly and realistically describes the divorce process and its effect on their lives and their child. It also shows from both viewpoints the difficulty, yet hope, of reconciliation. I had used the book as a counseling aid when people thought divorce was the answer and would end their problems.

The lady never returned for further advice. I thought maybe she considered my advice radical and not very professional. At least, that is what Old Sluefoot whispered in my ear: "You blew it again; look what you did to your nice lawyer image."

Two years later I met the lady again when we happened to be invited to a mutual friend's home for dessert and coffee.

She came up to me and said, "You don't remember me, do you?"

And although I'm usually pretty good with names and faces, I had to admit that I couldn't recall who she was. She reminded me of the time she came to my office for advice.

Sitting beside her now was her husband. She had taken my advice, and the marriage was reconciled.

"How exactly was your marriage restored?" I asked her, somewhat surprised by God's miracle.

"I met with several people weekly in a home prayer group," she said. "Every time we got together, we set up an empty chair that we believed my husband would one day occupy. We believed we would see him there.

"At each meeting," she continued, "we prayed for my husband. We put the chair in the middle of our prayer group and asked the Lord to fill it. We joined hands, prayed, and believed Matthew 18:19: 'If two of you shall agree on earth as touching any thing that they shall ask, it shall be done for them of my Father which is in heaven.' "

The woman told me that her husband didn't come back the next day. It took prayer and travail and concern by the entire prayer group.

Over a period of months God placed a desire in the man's heart for his wife and children. He came back to her and the marriage and family were restored.

Of course it wasn't easy. She had to forgive him even though he had hurt her so deeply. And he had to walk humbly before her and the Lord, having learned some things about the wages of sin.

But God brought them back together. Their marriage was healed, and it matured in the Lord.

God hadn't cast them aside because the husband had sinned. There was forgiveness and repentence, and God restored their marriage to the point that the husband and wife were truly one in the Lord.

The husband has now assumed the spiritual leadership of the home. He is respected in church, and husband and wife work together to help other couples in trouble.

But it wouldn't have happened if a Christian wife had not been willing to lay aside her hurts and let love cover the multitude of sins, as 1 Peter 4:8 says—and if other Christians had not encouraged and agreed with her in prayer.

When I start ministering reconciliation to someone, I don't know for sure what the results will be. The outcome is in God's hands. Many times if I had decided by appearances whether to even attempt reconciliation, I wouldn't have opened my mouth. But I discovered that with God all things are possible.

This truth became very obvious to me during the period I worked with Susan. She came to me for advice after her husband had filed for divorce.

The husband had left her and was living with another woman, but Susan still loved her husband and wanted to save the marriage.

I agreed to represent Susan—only I was not going to work for a speedy divorce as most lawyers would; I was going to work for reconciliation.

Through legal maneuvers I was able to stall the divorce proceedings to give God a chance to work on the husband. His lawyer called me and said, "John, what's going on? This is a simple divorce proceeding. Why don't you sign the papers to finish this thing?"

"Listen, Mike," I replied, "I think God can reconcile this marriage. My client is a Christian, and she is believing her husband will come back to her."

"Look, John," the other lawyer responded tersely, "my client has another woman now. Even the Good Book gives that as grounds for divorce."

"I still want to work for a reconciliation," I replied.

"This is crazy," he remarked. "You're not going to make any more money by stretching out the case. These people are not in a position to pay for extensive litigation."

"I still believe that God can reconcile the marriage;

and, the law provides for an opportunity for counseling. I'm going to file an answer that says that due to her Christian beliefs we're not going to admit that the marriage is irretrievably broken."

For the next nine months papers went back and forth between lawyers as I continued to stall.

The husband called the wife more than once, saying, "When are you going to let me go? Don't you understand I never loved you. I don't love you now, and I'm not going to reconcile our marriage. You have an idiot for an attorney, and you're an idiot too."

Despite the verbal blasts and the emotional wear and tear, Susan held firm.

But after nine months, nothing had changed, and she knew she was going to have to let her husband go. Just before Christmas she signed the final papers and had to tell her seven-year-old son his daddy wasn't coming home. Her two-year-old baby was too young to understand.

Although Susan had believed her marriage was going to be reconciled, her husband was now a "free" man. A few months later he married the other woman.

At this point almost anyone would give up all hope of reconciliation. Practically speaking, the man was gone forever.

And certainly his remarriage raised all sorts of theological questions.

But while onlookers and theologians might debate reconciliation theory, Susan continued to believe her husband would return.

He had known about the Lord. He was raised in church. But he hadn't seen much power in his traditional background to make him want to try God. And for him, when his marriage no longer was fresh, it was natural to look somewhere else for happiness.

Then he discovered that divorce and remarriage hadn't brought him happiness as he had hoped. God began dealing with him about his life and where real contentment is found. The stories he had heard about Christ and His love finally penetrated his heart.

Nine months after he divorced his first wife, he returned to her and divorced the other woman.

Susan, who had never given up hope, allowed her husband to return. He had said many cruel things to her in the past. He had violated their sacred marriage vows by committing adultery. But her forgiveness was greater than her husband's sins, and the marriage was reconciled.

God honored Susan's faith and brought her husband back to her.

I wasn't the main instrument of reconciliation in her marriage. She was. Without her deep commitment in God's standard, reconciliation wouldn't have worked.

It doesn't have to be a Christian lawyer who works as a minister of reconciliation. It can be a husband or a wife. It can be a concerned friend. It can be a whole church who teaches and practices reconciliation in relationships. People who commit themselves to reconciliation will see God move.

One thing I have learned while practicing reconciliation in marriages is that God is sovereign. We can't plug Him into our formulas and expect automatic results. Nor can we use Him to manipulate other people for our own purposes.

Proverbs 3:5-6 gives some wise counsel: "Trust in the Lord with all thine heart; and lean not unto thine own understanding. In all thy ways acknowledge him, and he shall direct thy paths."

When we earnestly seek Him, He will meet our needs in ways we can't imagine.

In another case I dealt with a woman who talked to me about her estrangement from her husband who was a lawyer and a nominal Jew.

She was a nominal Christian and a psychology major in college. Now she was a school psychologist. And she was facing a divorce.

When she and her husband were first married, they could not foresee that a divorce would be their eventual end. They were both very intelligent people. Certainly they could reason everything out. Slight religious differences should not be a handicap.

The wife had ignored or not been taught the admonition in 2 Corinthians 6:14; "Be ye not unequally yoked together with unbelievers: for what fellowship hath righteousness with unrighteousness? and what communion hath light with darkness?"

This woman was like so many others who hadn't applied God's principles to her life before she was married. Now she was suffering the consequences.

After she was married, she had become a committed believer in Jesus. Her love for Israel and for her husband grew. It didn't seem fair that her husband's love for her cooled, and he became involved with his secretary and was now asking her for a divorce. But life isn't always "fair" or "just."

Now she was trying to do all the right things to keep her husband and marriage. She confessed Matthew 18:19 as her verse. She prayed fervently for her husband and marriage.

She used Matthew 18:18 as a basis for binding Satan in her marriage and for loosing God's healing power to restore their union. But nothing changed.

She went to several pastors to have them pray for her marriage. She claimed in faith that the marriage was whole. Still, her husband wanted a divorce.

She had put her husband through three years of law school; she had helped him when he first struggled with his law practice. If anyone had a right to a good marriage, it was this woman.

Over a period of months I did everything I could to help reconcile the marriage. I talked with her husband repeatedly. I stalled the divorce proceedings. I interceded in prayer on her behalf. My wife prayed and counseled with her.

But the divorce was finalized despite all our efforts. God in His sovereignty did not change the husband's mind. That man had a free will, and God did not force him to reconcile with his wife.

God did do something else, however—something that showed His great love.

So often when a person has suffered through a divorce, Satan will move in for the kill. His weapons are feelings of bitterness, guilt, and shame.

I have seen many people lose their self-esteem because of the rejection that accompanies divorce. They keep believing they are total failures in life and that no one wants them. They often stop going to church because they feel judged and out of place.

I have also seen people live with feelings of deep guilt for what has happened, even when the divorce was not really their own fault. They feel totally rejected and believe they have failed God, failed their children, and failed others. They think their actions were the sole cause of the marriage dissolution. And no matter what others say, their sin hangs about their neck like a millstone dragging them into the pit of depression.

Another common aftermath of divorce is bitterness. If looks could kill, I would be handling many homicide cases. Satan uses the bitterness to keep the injured party wallowing in self-pity. He knows that a bitter person will no longer be a useful member of society—let alone of God's Kingdom.

God has defeated Satan, however. And in this woman's life Satan did not have the final victory. She continued to seek the Lord, and He healed her bitterness. Her Christian friends surrounded her with love, and her self-esteem was restored.

She accepted God's forgiveness and was no longer trapped in guilt. She grew in faith and wholeness.

God healed her life.

A short while ago God even showed this woman how complete her healing was.

She told me recently that she met her former husband and his new wife at a college football game. She stopped and chatted with them, not even thinking of the pain and deep hurts they had brought her.

It wasn't until after she said goodbye to her former husband that she realized what she had just done. She had felt no anger or animosity. There was no bitterness present. She didn't feel inferior or somehow cheated. She simply felt whole and secure in Christ.

God had done something beyond human understanding in her life.

There is no quick, automatic formula to bring about reconciliation. And not all spouses allow themselves to be reconciled. Some people choose to follow their own way and reject God's healing in relationships. But for those who truly want God's will for their lives, He will hear their cry and be their Comforter.

By the time I finally gave up the sixty percent of my law practice that dealt with divorce cases, I knew I had no alternative. I was a Christian called to practice reconciliation.

I realized that once I, as an attorney, accepted

money from one of the parties of a divorce, the other party viewed me as an enemy. I would no longer be able to be a mediator between the husband and wife. As an attorney I actually became a wedge.

Spouses who hire attorneys are instructed to no longer talk to each other. The attorneys talk for them and conduct the battle. Instead of two people having to agree, now there are four; and the chances are that three of the four are working for the divorce.

The adversarial process also becomes a financial wedge between the husband and wife, adding more strain to a shaky marriage.

As a young lawyer I liked nothing more than winning a case. I often said, "Winning isn't everything, it is *the only thing*." I would often repeat Churchill's quote, "We must not think of defeat; it is entirely out of the question." The adversarial relationship fit in very nicely with these goals of being number one in anything I did.

Historically, rich people decided who was right by hiring the biggest bully they could find to go against their opponent's biggest bully. The winner of the match would be the victor of the suit. Later, the arena changed, and intellectual combat replaced physical combat. I, as a lawyer, was an intellectual bully fighting for my client. Sometimes this meant separating spouses instead of reuniting them.

Over the years that I struggled with my spiritual predicament, God kept reminding me of Matthew 19:6: "What God hath joined together, let no man put asunder."

I argued with God that He had called me to be a good Christian lawyer, not a minister. This is a very shallow argument with God, believe me. After I would end my pragmatic dissertation, God would seem to reply, "John, one of us is going to change, and it isn't going to be Me."

Then He spoke to my heart as He had spoken to Job. "What is that to Me? I made the stars, I made the sun, I made the moon. I can take care of your law practice. I can give you other kinds of cases."

After several years of increased internal struggle on my part I finally totally surrendered my domestic practice to God. I determined not to be a wedge in marriages. Instead I would meet with parties for no fee and counsel them, allowing God to work His miracles in their lives.

Since the time I first began practicing reconciliation in marriages, I have seen over 100 married couples saved from the agony of divorce.

Second Corinthians 5:19 says that we are all ministers of reconciliation; yet we let some of our Christian friends divorce without ever confronting them. We are so "laid back" that we don't get involved. Satan tells us, "It's none of your business, and besides it is a messy, messy business."

If God could reconcile the world back to himself through Christ, then certainly we, Christ's Body, can work to reconcile marriage partners who are on the verge of divorce.

8

Prodigals

Several years ago a prominent Christian businessman called me for help. His fifteen-year-old son Tim was being held at the juvenile detention center, charged with participating in over twenty residential break-ins.

I sensed his urgency as he asked me to intervene on his son's behalf. I had known him and his family for about ten years. The parents had tried to follow the right Christian formulas for raising their children.

I knew, too, that the son had once been enrolled in a drug rehabilitation program. My heart went out to the distressed father, and I said I would see what I could do.

After arriving at the detention center, I talked to the boy and to the detective who was handling the case. I learned that Tim was the youngest member of a group of several boys who were under suspicion for the neighborhood burglaries.

The police, however, seemed more interested in punishing the older ringleaders than the fifteen-year-old.

Although there was some evidence against the boy, the legal case appeared weak. I talked again to the family and to the police and to the boy, trying to work out a way of freeing the lad.

After several telephone conversations between the detective and the state attorney's office, and after Tim promised to testify in any other burglary cases if needed, the charges against him were dropped. As a condition of his release, Tim was to be enrolled in a local rehabilitation program. The authorities recognized that he still had a drug problem. The young teenager had been in one of the most recognized and respected drug rehabilitation programs in the nation once before but had given up the program prematurely.

With the main crisis passed, I turned my attention to the family. I encouraged them to be loving and united as Christians, and I talked to the boy about turning his life around. I wanted him to change his peer group—which is easier said than done.

Their son needed help from Christian believers, but where? Their son needed people who would teach him spiritual warfare, love him, and stand with him. He needed to understand that drugs were an instrument of Satan in the battle for men's minds and that they would corrupt the body, God's temple. The young man needed to understand the consequences of man's disobedience of God's law and of God's tremendous love for each of us.

However, there was a battle going on for his body, mind, and spirit between a God of love and a Satan of deception. It was a raging war that every parent of a chemically dependent child knows all too well. It was a life and death matter that could not be ignored or covered with "sloppy agape."

This situation required mature Christian love that was willing to confront the problem head-on and required accountability on the part of all the parties. Tim's parents weren't up to the task, however. The father did not practice the tough love and commitment that this situation called for. The son's problem would not just go away—no matter how much it was ignored or wished away.

Everything that had worked with raising their two girls as responsible Christians was not working with their son. As the mother and father used the past tried-and-true approach, and failed, they became more and more despondent.

The parents now suffered the agony of having their son lie to them repeatedly. They had to face people who knew their son had a drug problem and was involved in thefts. They also needed love from the Body, *not* superficial judgment as though they were the only ones in the church with a problem.

The son did not want to turn his life around, and the father did not know what to do.

A year later I received an early morning telephone call from Tim. He was in jail again and wanted my help. This time I had a real conflict within, trying to know what to do. Should I try to get the young man off the hook again? Or should I do the thing that was really in his best interest?

Before I called Tim's father, I prayed for God's direction. About 6 a.m. I telephoned the father, "George, I'm really concerned for you and your family. I'm also concerned that your son never hears what you or I tell him.

"It seems to me," I continued, "that our actions speak louder than our words. When your son wanted to come home from the first drug rehabilitation program prematurely, you allowed him to do it. When he was arrested for the break-ins, you called me to get him out of trouble. I came to the rescue and he was freed. Later, when you told him how his life must change, there was never any follow-through to see that it did change. You took some of his privileges away, but it didn't affect him or change his friends. The threats and actions simply did not get the job done."

The father didn't interrupt my train of thought.

"I've prayed about what to do, and the Lord is giving me peace about telling you that I won't represent your son. I think I would be contributing more to the problem than to the solution. Our actions would be speaking louder than our words again. Your son will see it as, 'Dad is bailing me out again: I can always count on dad to get me off the hook. Even if he says he won't, he will.'"

I knew my words sounded harsh to the frustrated father. He was a man caught in a love trap. He didn't want his son to suffer, and over the years he had removed the penalties for his son's actions or had not had the time to enforce them consistently. He tried to gain his son's love by protecting the boy from his own consequences.

This story does not have a happy ending. The young man, who inwardly wanted discipline from his father, lost love and respect for his parents. The boy wanted a tough love—a love that could discipline and shape as well as protect.

But the parents were afraid to give this type of love

to their son until it was too late. They were afraid he would reject them.

Today "the thing they feared most has come upon them." The young man still is not reconciled to his parents. He continues to walk in disobedience and rebellion, and the family is emotionally broken—including parents, grandparents, and sisters. This type of problem affects the whole family. One member of a family can have a tremendous impact for destruction or healing of the entire family unit.

The parents could have learned a valuable lesson from the parable of the prodigal son in Luke 15.

The prodigal son demanded his inheritance from his father. He was still immature and simply wanted his own way.

The father could have refused his son's request. "After all," he might have reasoned, "it's a cruel world out there. My son isn't ready to be turned loose; he may be old enough, but he isn't mature enough."

Instead, the father realized he could not protect his son from life. He loved his son enough to give him his freedom; he allowed the boy to discover the consequences of his own actions.

It must have been extremely difficult for a loving father to give in to the foolish son's demands, knowing the boy would probably make some terrible mistakes and even squander the inheritance. But there comes a time when a parent can no longer protect a child from the world. A loving parent cannot keep a child in a bubble of protection forever.

Love demands freedom of choice.

Sure enough, the son made some terrible mistakes when he left home. He not only lost his money; he lost his happiness as well.

Luke 15:17 says that the boy finally "came to

himself" and thought of his father. He determined to return home and confess he had sinned.

The father, who loved his son greatly, received the prodigal back in his home with great joy. By releasing the son, he had actually won him.

And like the prodigal, some parents have to "come to themselves" too. They have to take some definite positive steps to change the course of their families.

So often parents are so wrapped up in themselves, their jobs, and desires that they don't see what the Father has to offer them. They are out in life, trying to make it on their own to become successful—while all the time a loving Father waits for them at home where there is peace, love, and security.

Prodigal parents breed prodigal children—especially in today's society—and some drastic steps are required to end the cycle.

First of all, the parents must do what the prodigal son did in the story. He came to himself.

Parents must honestly evaluate where they are. The Christian businessman whose son Tim was in the detention center had put his business before his family too often. While he was building a lucrative business, he didn't have time to meet his own family's demands. He took his family to church and did "Christian" things, but his Christianity was not seen in all the activities of his home life.

Parents must determine if they're really living for God or are actually living for themselves.

The second thing parents must do is come home and ask forgiveness.

It must have been very humbling for the prodigal to admit that he had made a terrible mistake. But it is to his great credit and reward that he made the admission. Parents must ask forgiveness too—not only of their heavenly Father but also of their earthly children.

It may be hard for parents to say to a child, "Billy, I've made a terrible mistake. Instead of putting you and mom first, I've been putting my business first. I was more concerned with having financial security for my family than I was with having your love. I didn't mean it to be that way, but it was, and now I'm going to change."

Howard

After the confession is made, the parents will then have to walk in repentance. Otherwise, the family will never learn real Christian confession and repentance.

The parents who were too busy with their own activities will have to devote *time* to their children.

Children who are given the leftovers realize it, even if they don't say it. Children are going to get your time and attention one way or the other. Freely giving it now is better than having to give it later when children are in rebellion. Also, your children *may* decide to give that time back to you when you need it so much in later years. You taught them this important lesson by actions rather than just words.

Parents can't give their children quality time when they are physically exhausted from their own activities. It's easy to say, "I give my children quality time; I don't have a great quantity of time to spend with them."

Somehow people seem to think that quality makes up for the lack of quantity. The next time you go into a restaurant, order the best steak in the house. Tell the waiter you don't care how much steak he brings you; you only want whatever he brings to be the very best. When he only brings you a one-half-ounce piece of meat, don't complain; you got quality. Remember that quality and quantity must both be present.

Real love is seen in vulnerability. Christ was vulnerable and won a lost world to himself. Parents must be vulnerable too if they are to win the love of their children. When parents allow children to see their mistakes, children can understand and forgive. But when parents cover their sins, they teach their children, by example, to cover their sins also.

It's hard for children to understand the spiritual love of God when they don't experience physical love from their parents. It is also difficult for children to believe God has time to listen to them, and wants to, when their earthly parents don't. They reason, "Maybe God has more important things to do; mom and dad always do."

Another thing prodigal parents must do is look forward instead of back. Satan will always be there to tell you how bad you are and make you feel guilty for the past. But remember, "Love covers a multitude of sins," as 1 Peter 4:8 says.

When parents are honest with God and themselves, they can be honest with their children. Reconciliation between parents and children is possible.

Recently a college professor and his wife came to me for help with their son who had been detained at school for possession of marijuana and drug paraphernalia.

The father was a professor at a local college, and the mother was a college graduate. They had read books on child rearing and knew what many textbooks said about dealing with drug problems. But their son still was in trouble.

I told the parents I wasn't there to try to get their son off; rather, I wanted to see a complete solution to the problem. I had finally learned a lesson from prior cases. I said, "I think we need a spiritual answer and not just a legal answer."

They agreed.

Under those conditions I agreed to accept their case.

I talked to the parents about the son's background. He had done exceptionally well in school during the grade school years. He was in the mentally-gifted program and was well liked by his classmates. However, when he reached junior high school, things began to change. His grades began to slip, and the parents noticed he had acquired friends who were not very well respected.

When he was thirteen, he had been arrested for prowling, but no action was taken. The parents were seeing warning signals that something was wrong and didn't know what to do. Instead of facing the issue with their child, they had ignored the problem, hoping it would go away.

They reasoned, "It's typical adolescence, and he is intelligent; he will grow out of it." They were afraid to confront their son in love and help him change; after all, they might fail.

But these parents were now willing to admit they were wrong. They were also ready to do whatever was necessary for their son to be helped. The parents made themselves vulnerable in order to help their son.

They opened the doors of communication by not judging their son for his actions. They also realized that consequences follow behavior. The problem was no longer ignored.

The case was placed in a juvenile arbitration program where the young man had a full hearing and learned what his actions meant and what options he had.

He had to face what he had done and make restitution and apologies. His parents and counselors helped him change. In a year's time the high school student overcame his chemical dependency with the help of his parents and a counselor. They loved him and kept faith in him during a residential treatment program. He no longer needed drugs, and he changed friends. His grades once again were excellent, and he was reconciled to his parents.

The change didn't happen overnight. It took time— time to change old patterns, time to heal wounds, time to build new relationships with parents and friends.

The boy's parents were willing to give their son a love commitment that would realistically help their child no matter what the cost to them personally or socially. And even when they did not agree with the counselor or rehabilitation program, the parents still supported the counselor and program and showed their son unified support. The result was refreshing to see.

So often Christians want instant answers to their problems. They pray and confess that the problem has disappeared. But God's ways are not necessarily our ways. Problems that have developed for years may take years to clear up.

During this time parents start realizing that the answer to the prayer may have to come through them. They themselves have to surrender to God in order to have their families healed; they have to be reconciled to the Father before their children will be reconciled back to them.

The answer to a parent's heartfelt prayers for a prodigal in trouble may begin in the Spirit the moment the parent is willing to do whatever is necessary to reconcile that child.

Christ doesn't want us to escape out of our problems. He wants us to walk through them and see that

He will change lives—ours as well as others—as we trust Him.

For the past eleven years I have been in close contact with a Christian home builder and observed how he raised his family. I always admired his relationship with God and his girls. I watched as he and his wife raised their two daughters, and I learned much about parenting from them. His youngest child was eight years older than my oldest child. And at the time we met, my oldest child was two.

"Earle," I asked the builder one day, "how did you get your daughters to turn out the way they did?"

He gave me a quick answer. "I gave them my time."

The answer sounded so simple, but I knew how hard it was to carry out. He didn't advertise as much as most successful businessmen do. He didn't have a large construction company, although I knew he had the ability to do whatever he set his mind to.

Instead he provided an adequate income for his family and gave his children something worth more than money—himself. He listened to his daughters when they wanted to talk to him about their hurts and desires. Sometimes he had answers for them and other times he simply shared their joys or tears. He prayed with his daughters almost every night. He shared the Word with them on a regular basis. He formed a relationship with them that was solid because he sacrificed his time.

Every Thursday night the family turned off the telephone, TV, and other modern distractions and had a family council. They simply spent time together as a family and communicated with one another as mother, father, and sisters. The girls were given an opportunity to share their complaints and gripes. By holding the family session once a week, they had time to reflect on the problems prior to presenting it to the family. The girls knew they would have the parents' undivided attention during that time—no newspapers or TV to compete with. Here was a weekly time for healing and reconciliation of the family.

Now his girls have reached their twenties. One works as a church secretary, the other attends college and works for a magazine. In both girls you can see the love of Jesus. Both girls believe Jesus is a reality and both love God.

They didn't have all the material trinkets that teenagers often want so much. They didn't have some of the material possessions that their friends had. But they had a father and mother who took time to love their daughters. Now both girls are prepared for life and are a joy to their parents.

It may have cost Earle some prestige in the community because he didn't build as many homes as other builders. And it no doubt was hard to make sure he was home at a reasonable hour each night so that he could be with his family instead of making a little more money.

But now, when other "successful" businessmen are seeing their dreams shattered because of rebellious children or by a wife who has possessions but not any love, Earle is secure. He is starting to reap the rewards for doing what the Word says.

His children honor him and his wife and love God.

He made it through the turbulent teenage years with his children because he had already established a pattern of love and trust in their lives when they were even younger.

To be reconciled to our children when they are still young eliminates fear of raising a prodigal.

9

Adoption or Abortion

"John, are you still interested in adopting a third child?" the obstetrician-gynecologist asked after I picked up the phone and said hello.

"Of course I am," I responded.

"Well, we've got a healthy baby that was born a few minutes ago at the Navy hospital, and if you want him, you can have him. But," he continued, "you've got to give me an answer within ten minutes, or I'll have to go through some other channels and give him to an agency to handle."

"How can this be, Bill?" I asked. "Why didn't you tell me before that you had a possible adoption coming up?"

"I didn't know before," the doctor responded. "This Navy trainee came in thinking she had the flu, and a few hours later she gave birth to a little boy! She wants to continue her Navy career and give the baby up for adoption. If you send one of your attorneys down right away to sign the papers, he's yours."

I couldn't believe what I was hearing. Carolyn and I wanted a third child to complete our family, but I thought it would be impossible. As a matter of fact, a few weeks earlier Carolyn had said she felt in her heart that we were going to get another baby soon, but I dismissed her thought, chalking it up to women's intuition.

As a ministry, our law firm helped people adopt children, and I knew there were no babies around to be adopted. The abortion plague that continues to sweep America had eliminated most adoptions.

"I'll send someone to sign the papers right away," I said.

I didn't even have to call Carolyn first to see if she agreed. A few hours later I could go home and surprise her.

"Honey, I have some news for you," I said nonchalantly when I got home. She expected a trivial, "I got rid of some junk in the garage."

Instead, I somewhat calmly said, "We're going to have a second son in two days."

Carolyn was elated! God had answered the faith He had placed in her heart several years earlier and confirmed only weeks before the birth.

After we got our new child, we discoverd how much of a miracle he really was. In examining the mother's medical records, our doctor came across some startling information. The mother had previously had an abortion. And she had taken two pregnancy tests at two different hospitals during her pregnancy with our new son Andrew. However, both pregnancy tests had turned up negative. If she had known she was pregnant again, she would have had another abortion.

God spoke quietly to my wife after we heard these surprising facts. "Carolyn, that's the reason he's named Andrew. Just like Brother Andrew smuggled so many Bibles to Christians behind the iron curtain, your baby was smuggled in just for you. I hid the truth from the doctors so that he would live."

We had seen God move on our behalf for us to adopt Andrew—the same as He had when we adopted each of our other two children earlier. Carolyn had always desired three children, and God had honored that desire and faith.

Before I was married, the subject of adoption had never seriously entered my mind. And after I was married in August of 1965, I assumed we would have children later on.

When the Vietnam War heated up, I decided we better have a child quickly. I was in law school and could continue to be deferred after graduation if I was a father. Being a calculated goal-setter, I thought that having a child in 1968, just before graduation, would be the pragmatic thing to do.

However, through no lack of interest or medical reason on our parts, Carolyn did not become pregnant before graduation. I accepted a direct commission in the Navy Judge Advocate General Corps to avoid the draft. Carolyn and I were disappointed, although for different reasons.

I approached the subject of fatherhood from a practical, almost businesslike, standpoint, but Carolyn deeply yearned to have a child. She had majored in childhood education and home economics in college. Her dream was to be a mother and homemaker.

Carolyn and I went through a broad battery of medical and fertility tests to see what was holding up our plans. They were embarrassing and frustrating.

During the medical testing I came to define a urologist as a doctor with a sadistic bent. Carolyn and I went through all of the tests and found out that basically we were normal. Some minor problems they discovered should not prohibit pregnancy.

After repeated lack of success, Carolyn explored other possibilities for having a family. She talked to me about adoption, and although I was not totally sold on the idea, I agreed to consider it because it was important to her.

We applied with a Christian mission home in Texas while I was in the Navy. As we waited for a baby, God worked in my heart. In late 1969 I surrendered my life to God and began growing in Him. In September of 1970, I received a phone call from the administrator of the mission home. He said our son had been born.

We received our baby in a chapel ceremony. Carolyn was excited and cried, and I wondered what I had gotten myself into. I was still a goal-setter, and by the time we got our new son Randy home after the ceremony, I had figured out how I could get him through college and how much it would cost.

God wanted to teach me more than what it means to be a provider for my family, however. He wanted to show me the greatness of the Father's love.

Romans 8:15-17 says,

> For you did not receive the spirit of bondage again to fear, but you received the Spirit of adoption by whom we cry out, "Abba, Father." The Spirit Himself bears witness with our spirit that we are the children of God, and if children, then heirs with Christ, if indeed we suffer with Him, that we may also be glorified together. (NKJV)

For the first time in my life I understood how much

our Father could love us, His adopted children. Although my new son Randy was not flesh of my flesh, God gave me a deep love for him when he entered our family. Sometimes I looked at him and tears came to my eyes because I loved him so much. I wanted to provide for him and protect him. I wanted him to understand what security really is.

I saw that we all belonged to God by the Spirit of adoption, and in my young Christian walk I began sensing the Father's great love when He sent His Son to reconcile the world back to himself. God gave much to gain many adopted sons and daughters.

Through Randy's adoption I also discovered a new love for people. I had a new understanding of the term, "brothers and sisters in Christ." We have *all* been adopted, and I sensed how deep the relationship with my adopted brothers and sisters could be. It could be as deep as my own love for Randy and as my Father's love for me when He sent His Son to "redeem" us.

Galatians 4:4-7 says:

> But when the fullness of the time had come, God sent forth His Son, born of a woman, born under the law, to redeem those who were under the law, that we might receive the adoption as sons.
>
> And because you are sons, God has sent forth the Spirit of His Son into your hearts, crying out, "Abba Father!" Therefore you are no longer a slave but a son, and if a son, then an heir of God through Christ. (NKJV)

Randy's adoption came at an important time in my personal and professional life, teaching me what compassion means. Compassion would help me minister to my clients' deep personal needs as I began my law practice. It would help me be sensitive and gentle to my family, too, placing their needs first.

God had other things to show me as Carolyn and I prepared to adopt a second child.

By this time we had both been baptized in the Holy Spirit and had encountered God's miraculous ways. God had allowed us to move to Orlando, Florida, to finish my Navy career. I was preparing for private practice, and Carolyn and I talked to various adoption agencies about having another child.

Many of them told us we were very fortunate to have one adopted child; it would be extremely unlikely that a second child would be placed in our home.

We seriously and continually prayed that God would provide us with another child. We didn't want Randy to grow up as an only child. I had been an only child and knew the unique problems of an only child.

Since being baptized in the Holy Spirit, Carolyn and I both discovered a new, more natural way to witness to people. We no longer had to rely on trick questions or pamphlets in order to discuss Jesus. He became a natural part of our conversation. We didn't know that God would use this "naturalness" as a link to adopting our second child.

In early 1973 Carolyn went to a doctor for a check-up. While she was there, she shared with the doctor how God was working in our lives and how we were trusting God for another child. Several months later the doctor called us and said he knew of a baby that was going to be placed for adoption as soon as it was born. He wondered if we would be interested.

We were!

We brought Julie home from the hospital on Mother's Day of 1973, and Randy had a new sister. It was the best Mother's Day present Carolyn ever received.

While Randy and Julie blessed our home, their lives also helped me discover joy in my law practice. In a profession where there are often long and sometimes bitter confrontations between prosecution and defense attorneys it was a joy to help other people adopt children.

In the adoption process it often seemed that everybody won. A baby who might have been killed through abortion was placed in a loving home. Adoptive parents who had an abundance of love to give could shower it on a new child. Natural parents who either could not raise the child or who totally refused to care for the child had the responsibility taken away.

As a personal-injury attorney I had all too often seen the aftermath of adoption's alternative—abortion. I recognized that abortion is not a nice, safe procedure. It is the killing of a fetus. It is the taking of a human life. In short, murder.

Our law firm worked with the National Right to Life organization to prevent abortionists from coming on the staff of local hospitals. We had worked to stop abortion clinics in our area. And we had counseled and aided guilt-ridden and injured girls who had suffered through an abortion only to discover that abortion did not end the problems. Often it left them with emotional scars and sometimes even permanent physical problems.

I knew abortion was not a panacea for society's problems. Abortion itself was a much worse problem. It directly violated God's most basic law concerning the sanctity of human life.

I had also heard humanistic arguments and often sensed that at the core of their arguments was a desire to allow man rather than God to determine who could live and who couldn't. It was also part of a concerted effort to make the state the sole decider of who could or couldn't have children.

Over a five-year period our law firm helped over 100 families adopt children. God's miraculous love flowed in these situations and created strongly bonded families.

This was in stark contrast to the personal-injury cases I had to handle when women had been seriously injured during abortions because they had been treated by less-than-qualified physicians in inadequate facilities.

And even if the facilities were adequate, I counseled women suffering from severe psychological problems because of an abortion. Often, teenage girls who were not mature enough to think through the consequences of abortion at the time they permitted it now suffered from severe guilt. Taking a life is a tragedy that stays in the mind and severely cripples many women—no matter what pro-abortionist forces claim to the contrary.

Women who were counseled to have an abortion were never told what Galatians 6:7 says: "Be not be deceived; God is not mocked: for whatsoever a man sows, that shall he also reap."

We never do escape the consequences of our actions, whether we are Christians or non-Christians. And those consequences include extreme guilt, self-condemnation, and a lack of self-esteem.

By comparison, I know many girls who decided to have the baby instead of getting an abortion. Although they were pregnant, they didn't compound their problems by having an abortion. These girls had the satisfaction of knowing that the child would be raised in a loving home with a mother and father.

In the same way that God gave His own Son so that

others might enjoy life, these girls gave a gift of joy to someone else by surrendering their child.

I have maintained contact with many of the mothers and the children they gave up for adoption over the past fourteen years. It confirms that the natural mothers made the right decision. All the children were placed in good homes where they were loved and quickly became a part of the family unit.

The mothers who surrendered their children to adoption resumed more normal lives. They were not faced with the guilt of having had an abortion. Many of them are now happily married. Some of them continued their schooling and established good careers. Perhaps they had made mistakes, but through counseling and love these girls discovered that there was hope. They weren't total failures, although Satan would like them to believe his lie. They recovered from their mistakes and are now productive members of society.

God moves in marvelous ways to heal people's lives. And I know He has a special concern for children—defenseless little ones who need love and security.

Sometimes I've stood in amazement, seeing God work things out according to His will when the adoption process looked hopeless. And I'm in awe of the great depth of human love that can flow to God's littlest children from Christians who are sensitive to the Spirit's voice.

One such demonstration of love occurred in a family in our commitment group which met monthly in one another's homes for prayer and fellowship. Six couples met and shared concerns and needs as well as joys and hopes. Men from diverse backgrounds brought their wives, and we all grew in a unity of the Spirit. One of these men was Dick, a purchasing agent for an electronics firm. He and his wife had three boys in a loving family.

However, Dick's wife Joanne had a desire for a little girl to complete their family. In her family background girls had been very important, and she felt a vacancy in her home because she didn't have a girl. Dick and Joanne wanted to fill this vacancy by adopting a little girl.

They asked me for advice, and I told them adoption was a long process and that there was no way to guarantee a possible adoptee would be a girl.

They prayed for God's help; the desire in Joanne's heart was especially strong.

One day I received a telephone call at the office from an older man concerned with the placement and custody of his six-month-old granddaughter. He had been referred to me by another attorney who knew of my personal and professional interest in adoptions.

The grandfather was considering the placement of his infant granddaughter for adoption—but only on his terms. He wanted to meet with and personally approve the adoptive parents and not leave this decision to my professional judgment. It was either his way or no way.

I told him this was not the way things are usually done. Normally prospective parents don't meet the adoptee's relatives. Too many complications can spring up to interfere with the adoption.

Later I told Dick and Joanne about the phone call, and despite my legal disclaimers and warnings, they insisted on going to meet the grandfather. They asked me to go along to help. I reluctantly agreed.

All the way to the grandfather's business I gave them all the right legal and practical reasons for not pursuing the adoption. But they were undaunted.

We met with the grandfather who had legal custody of the child. The girl's mother now lived in another state and had no contact with and showed no interest in her daughter; the father was physically unable to raise the child. It was up to the grandfather to make decisions about the child's future, with the father's consent.

Because of the grandfather's love and concern for the child, he insisted on meeting any prospective adoptive parents. He was in poor health and knew he had to make some decisions.

This proud, Italian grandfather wanted to make absolutely certain his little girl was placed in the right hands. He investigated Dick and Joanne's background and insisted on having several meetings together before making a decision.

During this entire period our commitment group prayed for God's direction. As the weeks passed, we all sensed the great love and concern that Dick and Joanne had for the little girl. Finally the grandfather agreed to allow the little girl to be adopted. We all rejoiced and thought the story had a perfect ending. But God had more.

Joanne found out that her new little girl had an older sister, and she began to pray that the two natural sisters would be reunited.

Dick and Joanne again approached the grandfather, asking for permission to adopt the older sister. But this time he was not willing. For almost two years Joanne prayed to have the second girl so that the sisters could grow up together.

Against the advice of her attorney (who had been wrong before), she maintained open relationships with her adopted daughter's father and grandfather.

It is almost always better to sever relationships

with former relatives and start life fresh for the adopted child, but Joanne went against what is normal because she felt she was doing God's will.

As I watched what was happening, I realized more than ever that no two adoptions are the same. God can move in any way He desires to bring about His plan.

Because Joanne continued a relationship with the grandfather and father, they actually got to see more of the little girl than they had before she was adopted. And Joanne showered them with kindness.

Finally, after two years of prayer and determination Joanne won the grandfather and father over enough that they allowed the older sister to live with her younger sister. She couldn't be adopted, but Dick and Joanne could have custody of her.

Later the grandfather died. The natural father knew he could not raise the second girl and signed the necessary papers for Dick and Joanne to adopt the older girl.

It had taken four years for Dick and Joanne to complete the adoption process, but they had assurance in their hearts that it would come about. Their Counselor was very familiar with adoptions and worked things according to His will. He is in the adoption business full-time, bringing many adopted sons and daughters into His Kingdom.

Two adopted girls now have three brothers and a loving mother and father to care for them. God created a beautiful family.

Adoption is a beautiful way to practice the ministry of reconciliation.

10

Life Sentence

In 1974, I met Roy, a young man charged
with first-degree murder. If found guilty, he could be
sentenced to death in the electric chair.

I visited him in jail while he awaited his trial. He
was a very agitated young man, nervous and edgy. I
tried to give him some legal advice and also share the
gospel with him.

Talking to him went against my grain. I had been a
Navy prosecutor for two years, and I didn't have time
for those charged with such serious crimes. Previously, as a trial attorney in the Navy Judge Advocate
General's Corps, I also had defended other murder
suspects, but it was hard for me. I felt that people who
committed serious crimes such as murder or rape
probably could not be rehabilitated and might deserve
even a greater sentence than they received.

As I walked out of the jail after meeting with Roy, I

was glad that a prominent local attorney had been appointed as special public defender so I didn't have to defend him. I not only didn't have time to help him; I didn't really *want* to help. I had done my Christian duty by telling him about Jesus. Now I could get on with more important matters in my law practice.

I walked out of Roy's life, but Jesus didn't give up on him as easily as I had. I was about to learn how deeply Christ's reconciling power reached.

I followed Roy's case with some interest during the following weeks because my secretary's husband happened to be involved in Roy's life. He and Roy had been from the same home town. As a Christian, he spent many hours counseling Roy while he was in jail.

Roy's case also had interest for me professionally because of another murder case in our area that was simultaneously making headlines. The cases were similar. But while Roy was a poor person, the murder suspect in the other case was the son of a very prominent attorney in the community. I, and the local media, wanted to see if justice would be meted out equally to rich and poor.

As it turned out, Roy's sentence was much more severe. While the other person received a minimum sentence, Roy got a life sentence. The newspaper and some people were upset with the different results, but nobody was surprised.

Originally, Roy had been charged with first-degree murder. His lawyer advised him to plead guilty to the lesser charge of second-degree murder for killing his girlfriend to avoid the possibility of the electric chair. The plea was entered, and Roy now began serving a mandatory minimum of twenty-five years in prison for the life sentence.

For the next two years I was reminded of Roy

whenever my secretary shared letters her husband had received from him. But the letters didn't really change my mind about him. He was serving time for a terrible crime he had committed, and I was not personally involved. I had plenty of clients with problems demanding my full attention.

Then four men I knew came to me with exciting news. They had gone to Raiford State Prison to conduct a weekend spiritual retreat for the prisoners. As a part of the "de Colores" spiritual outreach program, these men wanted to help the inmates.

And there was one man at the prison who really attracted their attention—Roy. He had surrendered his life to Christ and wanted to serve Him totally.

Since Roy had been in prison, he had taken many Bible correspondence courses. It seemed that Roy had fallen in love with the Word. He now had a string of certificates from several different Christian Bible correspondence schools, showing all the studies he had completed.

This was remarkable in itself because Roy had some prior psychiatric disorders. In 1963, when he was seventeen, he had been diagnosed as being schizophrenic.

When the judge had sentenced Roy in 1974, he even recommended that Roy receive psychiatric treatment, although this had not been carried out.

It was obvious to the four men that Roy was a changed person. While he was in prison, Christ had touched his mind and spirit. No longer did he bite his fingernails when he talked to people. No longer was he edgy and nervous. Roy had a personal encounter with Jesus. Now he flooded his mind with the Word, and Christ began a renewing process.

As his mind stabilized, he also caught up on his

education. He passed a graduate equivalency examination and received his high school diploma. Then he started taking college courses. He had already completed the first year of courses and was on his way to completing the second year.

The four men in my office continued to tell me about Roy. They wanted to help him. They felt that Christ helped Roy become rehabilitated.

"John, will you represent Roy?" one of the men finally asked. "Staying in prison isn't going to help him or society anymore."

Then the men agreed to pool their resources to pay my expenses. They gave me $400, thinking that the amount should cover the expenses. They had no idea that the time and legal work involved would be fifty times that amount if Roy had been a regular paying client. All they knew was that a Christian brother in prison needed help.

I agreed to represent Roy.

God had done something in his life that the prison system couldn't do—rehabilitate him.

I visited Roy and talked to him about God's power to help us change his circumstances. We wrote to each other, and he shared his life with me. Life in prison can be almost a literal hell, but Roy's Christian light shined there.

One day he wrote me, *"John, three days ago I helped an elderly man—one whom I've prayed for and preached to for two years. John, he shook all over and poured out his heart to Chaplain Martin and myself in tears. He confessed Christ, and is this night reading his Bible. Praise God."*

I took the necessary legal steps to help Roy.

At my insistence the prison officials who had not given him the psychiatric help that the sentencing judge had recommended interviewed him to consider giving him psychiatric treatment at the state hospital.

They didn't know that since Jesus had come into Roy's life, he had been healed. However, three of the best psychiatrists in the state tested Roy and declared that he was now sane.

I continued to work on Roy's behalf and in 1977 filed a motion with the judge who had sentenced him. The motion asked to reduce or abate his sentence.

On the last day before the judge retired from the bench, I had an hour-long hearing on Roy's behalf.

I filed the motion on the fact that Roy had not received psychiatric treatment as the judge had originally recommended. Instead, the State Department of Parole and Probation had sent him to prison for a minimum of twenty-five years, which was not the judge's intent. The judge had even sent a letter to the Department of Parole and Probation, stating that he was not necessarily in favor of lengthy incarceration even though Roy had been given a life sentence.

Also, the motion reminded the judge of the similarity between Roy's case and the other murder case that had been decided the same day that Roy's had been in 1974. The other man had been paroled shortly after he was sentenced.

My motion was vigorously opposed by the state attorney's office because of the severity of the charge for which Roy was serving time.

But on the basis of the hearing, the judge reduced Roy's sentence to twelve years. Because Roy had already served three years and 295 days, he became eligible for parole a short time later.

Roy was thirty-one years old and ready to start a new life.

After he was released, he went to work for a large electrical contractor as a journeyman electrician. Later he married a probation counselor and became involved in a church. Roy now has his own electrical contracting business.

God hadn't written him off in 1974 when I and most of society had.

After the judge reduced Roy's sentence, Roy wrote me a letter of thanks:

Dear John,

From time to time I've heard the question asked of people, "What would you do if you had your life to live over?" Earnestly, how does one answer such a question? Could I be less critical, would I be more selfless, do more for others? How about the time spent trying to impress others when really deep down I was crying for help—could I ever consider giving to others and share my concepts of logic and gift of Bible learning?

John, the biggest question is, "How does a man thank another man for his own life?" I've walked the floor and prayed for the answer, but it's simply not that simple. If these words are correct, and I feel they are, "Amazing Grace" is all I can say.

I know I only have the power to change anything in my life through the Lord Jesus! I'll work for Him the remainder of my life because I know He's so real and alive.

Thank you, Brother and instrument of God. I love you, Brother.

Roy

Roy's letter pierced my heart. How *does* a man thank another man for his life?

How could I thank Jesus for giving me my own life when He sacrificed himself on the cross? Roy's answer was appropriate—"Amazing Grace."

I, like Roy, wanted to work for Jesus the remainder of my life because of what He had done for me.

My experiences with Roy showed me how far-reaching the ministry of reconciliation should be. Often during the long hours of preparation and work on Roy's case I had wondered if my work was worth the effort. I was giving up precious time that could be spent on my law practice while helping a man at virtually no cost.

But I was continually reminded of Matthew 25:33-40:

> And He will set the sheep on His right hand, but the goats on the left. Then the King will say to those on His right hand, "Come, you blessed of My Father, inherit the kingdom prepared for you from the foundation of the world: for I was hungry and you gave Me food; I was thirsty and you gave Me drink; I was a stranger and you took Me in; I was naked and you clothed Me; I was sick and you visited Me; I was in prison and you came to Me."
>
> Then the righteous will answer Him, saying, "Lord, when did we see You hungry and feed You, or thirsty and give You drink? When did we see You a stranger and take You in, or naked and clothe You? Or when did we see You sick, or in prison, and come to You?"
>
> And the King will answer and say to them, "Assuredly, I say to you, inasmuch as you did it to one of the least of these My brethren, you did it to Me." (NKJV)

The Lord used this incident to impress me with the importance of each individual. He died for each one of us, whether we were on death row or whether we were lawyers or judges.

I realized more fully that being a minister of

reconciliation meant taking that reconciliation into the toughest spots in life—into places that most Christians never walk. It meant soiling our hands in the dirt of life. It meant helping those who are less fortunate than we.

James 1:27 has direct application to those wanting to practice reconciliation: "Pure religion and undefiled before God and the Father is this, To visit the fatherless and widows in their affliction. . . ."

I knew I could not reach everyone. I had learned my lesson about being over-extended. But I could reach some. I could reach those in my sphere of influence. Too often Christians see so many needs that they don't know where to start. They end up doing nothing.

I cannot help every orphan. I cannot help each person in prison. I cannot even help all the hurting Christians in my own church.

But I can do something.

Jesus spent most of His years of ministry with twelve others. If I and every other Christian touched twelve others intimately, the world would be changed.

The four men who asked me to help Roy were ministers of reconciliation. They dared to get dirty by going into a prison. They knew they could not do everything, but they could do something. They were just four average men. One was an insurance salesman, one was a donut shop owner, one was a vegetable broker, and one was a TV announcer.

They didn't know any law. They just knew there was a need. And they responded to that need. As a result, a young man whom God loves is now out of prison and is a servant of Jesus in his own community.

Roy was in a prison system that offers very little hope to inmates or society. The prison system in America is in such desperate need of reform that I don't believe Americans will be willing to spend the vast sums of money and effort necessary to change it. He had virtually been lost in the bureaucracy and might never have gotten any help if four Christians had not been sensitive to others' needs.

Not everyone can minister to prisoners, but I know many lawyers who can. If Christian lawyers took more time to present Jesus to their clients, some real reform could take place.

Quite frankly, prisoners who accept Christ in prison often have a very difficult time. They are looked on as weaklings and are no longer considered "macho." Often they are the object of jokes and even physical abuse. But when God intervenes in the seemingly hopeless prison cell, the convert knows the greatness of God. Roy knew, and he wasn't ashamed to tell others about it, regardless of what they thought.

As a result, he became a minister of reconciliation in prison and won others to Christ. It's surprising how people who are reconciled want to help others become reconciled also. Roy's release from prison was also a witness to other inmates of the power of Jesus to help them. His testimony remains in the prison even though he is no longer there.

Ministers of reconciliation have to reach others no matter where they are in life. Christ did the same for us.

Romans 3:23 says, "All have sinned and come short of the glory of God." While some Christians have resorted to classifying sins as bad and not so bad, in God's eyes we are all sinners. We all need a good lawyer to get us out of our dilemma.

One of the sayings among lawyers is, "Some lawyers know the law, and some lawyers know the judge." The implication is that it might be better for a client to get a lawyer who is a personal friend of the judge than to get one who only knows the law. This has not been my experience, but I have heard lawyers who just lost a case lament, "The other lawyer knew the judge."

All of us who are sinners need the right lawyer to plead our case before the Righteous Judge. In Jesus Christ we have a lawyer who knows the law *and* the Judge. Christ came to fulfill the law, and the Judge is His own Father. You can't do better than having a lawyer whose daddy is the judge.

Not only that, Jesus is above reproach. First John 2:1 states, "If any man sin, we have an advocate with the Father, Jesus Christ the Righteous."

If Jesus could humbly represent us to the Father through His sacrifice on the cross, certainly we can humbly reach others also and bring them into God's full forgiveness and healing—no matter what they have done.

11

Steps to Reconciliation

Many people coming to me for help are trapped in a problem with someone they love, not knowing how to extricate themselves. Many of them have let some incident in their lives get out of control. Now they can't bring it back into balance.

Sometimes small things have grown so out of proportion that they dominate the relationship. Thoughtless words or actions have destroyed relationships between friends, fellow workers, spouses, and brothers and sisters in Christ. The trapped people don't know how to be reconciled. Many don't even think reconciliation will work.

When people are faced with a problem, their common response is to look for someone to blame—"It's my employer's fault ... my wife's fault ... my parents' fault ... my teacher's fault." Many of my clients have said, "Look what they did to me ... said about me . . . took from me."

To begin reconciliation, however, the right response must be to realize the solution begins in me—not others. I can't change others, but I can change myself. People who want relationships restored must start by examining themselves.

For restoration to take place three steps are necessary: be reconciled to God, be reconciled to yourself, be reconciled to others.

Reconciled to God

The first step to complete reconciliation requires that we be honest enough to admit there is a problem.

If we have done something that we know is wrong, we must ask God's forgivensss. And it is hard, even for Christians, to admit being wrong.

We sometimes confine God to our religious box. In our concepts that God is a God of mercy, we forget that He is also a God of justice.

First John 1:9-10 says, "If we confess our sins, he is faithful and just to forgive us our sins, and to cleanse us from all unrighteousness. If we say that we have not sinned, we make him a liar, and his word is not in us."

In order for us to receive God's merciful justice, we must come to His court, asking forgiveness. And because we have an advocate with the Father, we will win the final case and receive an eternal reward.

But if we don't ask forgiveness, we are doomed to wallow in sin's consequences. We remain spiritual failures, being overcome by the world's problems instead of overcoming the world.

Not only must we ask God's forgiveness when we've done a wrong; we must ask for forgiveness from the person we've wronged. We do the asking, and the wronged person does the forgiving.

In my own life I have had to ask myself, "What have I done wrong and what can I do to restore the relationship?" The fact that the other person may have committed the greater wrong does not exempt me from initiating reconciliation by asking the other person's forgiveness.

It is much easier to forgive someone than to ask their forgiveness. *Important*

Very often we hold grudges or harbor resentment against someone who has hurt us. This is just as much a sin as if we were the one committing the wrong. When this is the case, we should simply tell God how we feel and why we feel the way we do.

He understands.

When we pour out our hurts to God, He then replaces them with His peace.

Reconciled to Yourself

Christians realize they have to be reconciled back to God. When they ask Jesus to forgive them of their sins, they discover that God's reconciliation works.

But while it is one thing to have God forgive us of our sins, it is quite another thing to forgive ourselves. Many people have discovered that God loves them. Now they have to learn to love themselves.

Many Christians' self-esteem is terribly low. They somehow have not come to the place of seeing how precious they are to God. They even wonder how God could love such a person as themselves. They're amazed that God forgave their sins in the first place. After all, they still make mistakes, they hurt and are hurt by others; they are not perfect.

"Ye are complete" in Christ, Colossians 2:10 declares. But many Christians don't realize that. They try to get their completeness through acceptance by family members or friends. They try to be complete by being respected as successful businessmen or home-makers. They try to be complete by belonging to church and being active as Sunday school teachers or deacons.

When we look to others to shape our self-image, we never will be reconciled to ourselves. The world equates being reconciled to yourself with being successful, but many people have sadly discovered that worldly success does not guarantee internal peace.

People who have not been reconciled to themselves continue to seek outside approval for their actions. They don't function from a base of security. Instead, their insecurity makes them do things they later regret.

They may fly off the handle easily when someone gets too honest with them or offers some constructive criticism. They don't have enough security as a person to face an issue calmly and directly.

Many people who have not been reconciled to themselves find their lives become lies. They have to brag about what they do or exaggerate their accomplishments so that others will think more highly of them. Then they feel guilty for lying, and their self-image drops even further.

People who are not reconciled to themselves worry a great deal what other people think of them. They have fertile imaginations and think that others are talking about them behind their backs or judging them. Somehow they can't cast down their imaginations and bring into captivity every thought to the obedience of Christ, as 2 Corinthians 10:5 directs.

In my own life being reconciled to myself was one of the hardest lessons I had to learn. I had always been taught to be a success and that fulfillment consists of

what other people think of you. From being the cap-
tain of the high school football team to becoming a top
academic graduate in college and law school, I worked
for others' recognition.

When I became a Christian, I carried the same
principles into my business career. As a Christian
lawyer, I wanted to be the best Christian lawyer in the
nation. I wanted to have a successful Christian practice not only as a witness to the world but also because
I needed recognition by others in order to feel secure.

I depended on a large income and the recognition of
men to let me know I was successful. I hadn't trained
my ear for God's confirmation, "Well done thou good
and faithful servant."

I had to learn that God elevates us; we don't have to
elevate ourselves.

If I had been honest, open, and vulnerable with God,
He would have helped me be reconciled to myself
much earlier in my life. Instead I sometimes adopted
the world's standards of success in my own Christian
walk.

I would like to say that in one glorious mountain-top
experience I became reconciled to myself and no
longer needed the "praise of men" in order to feel
accepted. However, my experience has been one of
gradual growth. God deals with me daily, item by
item, making me look more to Him for my security
rather than to things.

I have had to let go of things many times so that I
would not get puffed up in my own eyes. I clearly
remember the Lord's dealing with me over my position as director of the county bar association. I knew
that I would move up the association ladder to become
the president of the bar association in three years.

However, I refused to be nominated again, not

because the position was wrong, but because my praise was coming from men more than it was coming from God. In that particular position I was trying to elevate myself instead of letting God elevate me; when I refused the position again, I felt God's peace.

Later, God even dealt with me to cut down my case load and trust Him more for my financial security. Again, my security was not to come from outside sources; it was to come from God. As I discovered who I was in Christ, I didn't need as many external rewards to give me peace. When I became reconciled to myself, Jesus became my peace, as it says in Ephesians 2:14: "For He is our peace, who hath made both one, and hath broken down the middle wall of partition between us."

As I have counseled with people, one of the major problems I have seen in hurting Christians' lives is that they are not reconciled to themselves.

Many Christians who have great natural ability start applying external ways of achieving success. They haven't become secure enough to say no to the many voices around them calling for their time. They feel that if they don't help every person or cause that asks for their assistance, they are failing God.

These people often carry many Christian titles such as Sunday school superintendent and get their approval by people's praise.

They equate Christian jobs with spirituality and feel guilty if they cannot do whatever people ask them to do.

People who have not been reconciled to themselves can become devoured by religion. When they are not elevated to the next religious position or when they feel that their service hasn't been adequately recognized, they are deeply hurt.

I have known many of these people to leave the church and hold resentment against anything having to do with a particular denomination or local church.

They have felt man's rejection, and because it takes place in a religious setting, they think it is God's rejection as well.

If their rejection would have happened in the business world, they could have blamed working conditions or personality differences, but when rejection occurs in a religious setting, there is no one to blame. They can't blame God or God's servants; it must be their own fault. It is far easier to change jobs than to change gods.

Insecure Christians force each other to work even harder for approval. More witnessing campaigns are scheduled. More services are held. More special programs are implemented.

Christians who are not reconciled to themselves often work themselves toward a nervous breakdown, trying to experience God's peace through works alone.

Jesus says, "Peace I leave with you, my peace I give unto you: not as the world giveth, give I unto you. Let not your heart be troubled, neither let it be afraid." But some Christians are so busy trying to find peace through external acts that they don't have time to read John 14:27 to discover Christ's promise.

A person who has been reconciled to himself can dare to say no and suffer the consequences. It becomes a decision of what he desires more—the praises of men or the praises of God.

A person who can say no can also say yes to the right things. He discovers fulfillment in serving Christ in the position that Jesus has placed him. He may end up as Sunday school superintendent, but it will be in God's timing and not because someone else has exerted a religious "guilt trip" on him.

To be reconciled to yourself, you must accept yourself right where you are. You must accept all of yourself, including your physical appearance. Psalm 139:14 declares, "I will praise thee; for I am fearfully and wonderfully made; marvelous are thy works; and that my soul knoweth right well."

God has made you to be "wonderful." Accept that. It might be a good idea to stand in front of a mirror and thank God for each and every part of your anatomy. Thank Him for your "bad" features as well as your "good" features. He has made you, and He knows what He is doing. You are totally "wonderful" in His sight. To be reconciled to yourself, you must accept your physical self.

Once you accept your physical self, He can help you adjust what needs adjusting. If you go by the world's standards of what is physically acceptable, you will be frustrated most of the time. There are very, very few perfect physical specimens in the world, and even they age and change as the rest of us do.

The next thing you must accept is your mental self. Perhaps you don't have as much education as your spouse or your friends, but remember, your place in God's Kingdom will never be determined by a college degree.

When Christ saved us, He gave us access to His mind. Paul says in 1 Corinthians 2:16, "But we have the mind of Christ," and in Philippians 2:5, "Let this mind be in you, which was also in Christ Jesus." That mind is far wiser than any worldly mind.

Ask God to give you His wisdom, and be sensitive to His thoughts as you pray and read His Word. As you pray and feed on His Word, you will grow mentally.

Important

Accept your mental capacity, and stop apologizing for your lack of understanding or vocabulary. "Let no man deceive himself. If any man among you seemeth to be wise in this world, let him become a fool, that he may be wise. For the wisdom of this world is foolishness with God. For it is written, He taketh the wise in their own craftiness. And again, The Lord knoweth the thoughts of the wise, that they are vain. Therefore let no man glory in men" (1 Cor. 3:18-21).

When you accept yourself mentally, you can start hearing how God wants you to increase your knowledge. You get your eyes off mental recognition by man's standards and begin preparing yourself mentally in the way that God wants to use you.

He may call you to further study or education; He may tell you to read the newspaper more so that you can be a better witness to your news-oriented next-door neighbor.

When you surrender your mental capacity to God's leading, He can prepare you better than you ever could yourself. He knows your future much better than you do.

To be reconciled to yourself, you must also accept your spirit. First Corinthians 6:17 says, "He that is joined unto the Lord is one spirit." Many Christians are insecure because they don't recognize the unique union between the Spirit of Christ and their own spirit. They are married and don't live in all its benefits.

Insecure Christians try to work out their own spiritual destinies, not realizing that when they try to do spiritual things in the flesh they are simply being carnal.

When a person accepts Christ into his life, his spirit is made alive unto God. God's Spirit bears "witness with our spirit that we are the children of God," Romans 8:16 tells us.

However, we sometimes look to religion for the answers to our problems rather than to God's Spirit. The result is that we live a religious rather than a spiritual life.

And religion, which operates through law, kills. It is the spirit that gives life, 2 Corinthians 3:6 says.

When we are reconciled to our spiritual calling, we can serve God in newness of life.

I have seen many Christians whose lives were falling apart because they never used the power of the Spirit in their lives. Once they were born again, they tried to work out their salvation through their own acts.

One of the things that hurts me most is when people come to me for marriage counseling whose homes are in chaos because the parents are living religious lives. Instead of ministering to their families, they are doing all sorts of religious services for other people. They somehow can't hear God telling them that they first of all must be spiritual right in their own home.

Important

When a person gets his own life reconciled to God, he is ready to operate in the true ministry of reconciliation, bringing life and healing to others.

Reconciling to Others

Christians who practice the Word and walk it out in their everyday lives are strong witnesses to non-Christians.

Jesus said, "By this shall all men know that ye are my disciples, if ye have love one to another" (John 13:35). And when non-Christians see that reconciliation between brothers and sisters works, they are attracted to the reality of the gospel.

The world's system for reconciliation between

people is through the law. And then there is often an ulterior motive behind the reconciliation. Usually the reconciliation takes the form of settlement rather than healing. The parties agree to co-exist, but bitterness and resentment often continue.

For example, the two parties may come to a settlement on the exact amount still owed by one party to another on a disputed piece of property. But while a settlement is reached, the two parties have actually become more embittered in the course of the litigation. For years they may not talk to each other or, worse yet, publicly criticize each other or actually try to ruin each other in future business deals.

The world cannot reconcile their differences because they have no foundation of love on which to build. But Christians have a foundation.

Christians who have been reconciled to God and to themselves can be reconciled with others. Reconciliation doesn't work in the world because of selfishness; reconciliation should work in Christians' lives because of surrender.

It is a hard thing to surrender our rights, but that may be just what is required in order to have reconciliation.

A husband may have to surrender his right to go bowling or golfing with the guys; his wife needs him to help paint the living room.

A wife may have to surrender her right to browse through magazines or to go shopping with a friend; her husband needs several shirts ironed.

A child may have to give up playing with some buddies after school; the garage needs cleaning.

Great court battles have been fought over people's rights. I have handled many marriage dissolution problems which ended up as a fight over certain rights—demands to see the children every weekend, the right to keep the new boat, the right to receive alimony, the right to keep the house, the custody of the family dog, the college football season tickets, etc.

As U.S. citizens we declare that one of our "unalienable rights" is the "pursuit of happiness." And people today in America are pursuing happiness a great deal. But happiness is rather illusive. Having more things and obtaining more rights does not guarantee happiness.

As Christians we know that happiness comes in great measure by living in peace with others. We can dare to go to our brothers and sisters and ask forgiveness. We can be reconciled because God has joined us to each other as one Body.

When the world sees our unity, so unlike their competition, they are perplexed—but they want what we have. When we as Christians become reconciled to each other, we can reach the world with the ministry of true peace.

12

Let the Healing Begin

A recent survey in Albuquerque, New Mexico, revealed that one out of five court suits has a Christian taking another Christian to court.

The world sees this and remembers our actions rather than our words. We are the Bible that they read, and unfortunately our lives often do not line up with the Word.

Matthew 5:23-24 says, "If thou bring thy gift to the altar, and there rememberest that thy brother hath ought against thee; leave there thy gift before the altar, and go thy way; first be reconciled to thy brother, and then come and offer thy gift." Too often, however, we stay at the altar, pretending everything is fine. We forget that the world can read us like a book.

Matthew 18:15-18 gives even more complete instructions:

> Moreover if thy brother shall trespass against thee, go and tell him his fault between thee and him alone: if

he shall hear thee, thou hast gained thy brother. But if he will not hear thee, then take with thee one or two more, that in the mouth of two or three witnesses every word may be established. And if he shall neglect to hear them, tell it unto the church: but if he neglect to hear the church, let him be unto thee as an heathen man and a publican. Verily I say unto you, Whatsoever ye shall bind on earth shall be bound in heaven: and whatsoever ye shall loose on earth shall be loosed in heaven.

Instead of binding men together in Christian love, however, we have tried to bind them to a court's rules. The world sees our actions and believes there is no power or difference in Christianity.

In addition, many churches do not have the courage for their members to "tell it to the church." Instead of teaching or counseling the basic truths of reconciliation, the pastors or preachers advise, "This is a legal matter; get a good lawyer and tell it to the court."

I have known of a situation in a large church where the husband was being counseled about the family's domestic problems by one associate pastor, and the wife was receiving spiritual guidance from another associate. The husband attended the late morning service and the wife suffered through the early service. There was never any confrontation, accountability, or reconciliation sessions with the individuals and pastors. "Sloppy agape" carried the day. Two Spirit-filled Christians were divorced and never had to face the basic truths of the gospel or the responsibility for their actions.

The church continued to hold glorious, exciting praise services with salvation messages while the individuals attended separate services before, during, and after the divorce. Somehow, someway, I think the apostle Paul would have done something differently.

The modern church needs the return of men of courage and conviction to institute and practice the ministry of reconciliation—men like Paul and Peter who had been in the real world and could meet problems head-on.

This would be a change from the church where the pastor fears strong men of courage and convictions and often appoints weak men and women to important positions and committees in the church. This results in a church with one head rooster, a lot of hens, and a lack of true masculinity.

Reconciliation takes guts; fighting in court only takes lawyers.

Reconciliation means Christians have to admit they aren't perfect. They cannot hide behind spiritual platitudes and ignore the Word. The Word says to be reconciled. That means a Christian might have to expose his faults to another Christian. And that is hard to do.

It is easier to enter a court of law and let a lawyer do our fighting for us than to humble ourselves before our brothers so that healing and forgiveness can occur.

It is easier to say "amen" and "hallelujah" in church than to get rid of spiritual pride. It is easier to wear a Christian mask than it is to change.

The world can't understand our actions. They ask, "If Christians really believe the Bible, why don't they practice it?"

The church I attend has set up a service to help Christians reconcile disputes rather than take them to court. We call it a reconciliation ministry, and it has worked well in its first year of operation—sometimes to the amazement of all of us.

This service is available to any member who has a legal dispute or disagreement with another member. It also can be used by a non-member who has a legal problem with a member of our church, as long as both parties agree to have the issue decided scripturally by three qualified Christian arbitrators.

I believe a reconciliation ministry needs to be set up in churches from coast to coast in order to make a difference in this nation. I also believe the long-neglected scriptural teachings on reconciliation and restoration need to be boldly taught to the members in a concerted, practical way. Then they can understand and apply it to their everyday lives. If the ministry of reconciliation is going to work, it has to reach the entire Body in Christ. It has to start with each of us in individual churches—now.

The Christian Legal Society (CLS) initiated Christian Conciliation Services with a pilot project in May, 1980. A conciliation service is now available in twenty-three metropolitan areas to settle disputes between Christians regardless of denominational background.

As a member of CLS, I support the ministry of the Christian Conciliation Service; however, it is only a small part of what we could all do to reach the Body with the ministry of reconciliation.

We need reconciliation throughout the Church, nation, and world. We can't afford to wait for an excellent project; it needs to start in the lives of individuals and churches immediately.

Matthew 18 gives specific instructions on how to reconcile, and churches can help their members follow the Word. It is very difficult for some Christians to confront others with whom they disagree. Often there are walls of bitterness standing between the parties.

It is often easier for Christians to change churches than to confront and reconcile an issue with another member. This is why each church needs its own conciliation ministry to teach its members the spiritual truth of reconciliation.

A church that is concerned about the ministry of reconciliation can help its members come together to resolve their differences.

The apostle Paul had some very strong words for the Corinthian church because it was not practicing the ministry of reconciliation among its members. His words apply just as much today:

> Dare any of you, having a matter against another, go to law before the unjust, and not before the saints? Do ye not know that the saints shall judge the world? and if the world shall be judged by you, are you unworthy to judge the smallest matters? Know ye not that we shall judge angels?
>
> If then ye have judgments of things pertaining to this life, set them to judge who are least esteemed in the church. I speak to your shame. Is it so, that there is not a wise man among you? no, not one that shall be able to judge between his brethren? But brother goeth to law with brother, and that before the unbelievers.
>
> Now, therefore, there is utterly a fault among you, because ye go to law one with another. Why do ye not rather take wrong? Why do ye not rather suffer yourselves to be defrauded? Nay, ye do wrong, and defraud, and that your brethren.
>
> Know ye not that the unrighteous shall not inherit the kingdom of God? Be not deceived; neither fornicators, nor idolaters, nor adulterers, nor effeminate, nor abusers of themselves with mankind, nor thieves, nor covetous, nor drunkards, nor revilers, nor extortioners, shall inherit the kingdom of God.
>
> And such were some of you: but ye are washed, but

> ye are sanctified, but ye are justified in the name of the
> Lord Jesus, and by the Spirit of our God (1 Cor. 6:1-11).

The apostle Paul recognizes the fallen state of man. No one is good enough to judge someone else in that state. But when we became Christians, we took on Christ's character and righteousness. Now we are to use that character and righteousness to help each other be reconciled.

Our tendency is to ignore problems, hoping they will go away. But they don't go away. They may be hidden for a time, but they will emerge again and probably be even more severe.

Christians often see other Christians who have problems with each other, but the observers pretend it is none of their business. They are afraid to interfere lest someone thinks they are "snooping."

These observers even stand on Scripture: "Judge not, that ye be not judged. For with what judgment ye judge, ye shall be judged: and with what measure ye mete, it shall be measured to you again. And why beholdest thou the mote that is in thy brother's eye, but considerest not the beam that is in thine own eye?" (Matt. 7:1-3).

Christians who judge other Christians certainly must look at their own lives first and consider their own motives. If they are judging others and condemning their actions so that they themselves look more spiritual by comparison, they are hypocrites and living in sin. But if Christians judge each other through eyes of compassion so that disputing brothers and sisters can be reconciled, then they are following the Word.

"Brethren, if a man be overtaken in a fault," Galatians 6:1 says, "ye which are spiritual, restore such an one in the spirit of meekness; considering thyself, lest thou also be tempted.''

It seems, according to Galatians 6:1, that if we don't try to reconcile our brothers and sisters, we might end up with the same problems they have.

Satan works hard to separate and destroy the body of Christ through distrust, fear (including rejection), and lies. He still tries to control the Christian's mind, planting seeds of doubt and insecurity.

We Christians are in a spiritual warfare with Satan. We must fight the enemy of our souls and not each other. I personally have my hands full of problems with Old Sluefoot without having to look for additional struggles.

Christ prayed, ''That they all may be one; as thou, Father, art in me, and I in thee, that they also may be one in us: that the world may believe that thou hast sent me'' (John 17:21).

As Christians are reconciled to each other, they become an answer to that prayer.

When Christians are in one accord, some mighty things take place.

> And when the day of Pentecost was fully come, they were all with one accord in one place. And suddenly there came a sound from heaven as of a rushing mighty wind, and it filled all the house where they were sitting.
>
> And there appeared unto them cloven tongues like as of fire, and it sat upon each of them. And they were all filled with the Holy Ghost, and began to speak with other tongues, as the Spirit gave them utterance (Acts 2:1-4).

Christians who want to restore power to their church must be in ''one accord,'' and that accord comes as we are reconciled to each other.

Being in one accord takes time (and hard work). No doubt the 120 disciples who gathered in the upper room on the Day of Pentecost had to get a few things straightened out among themselves. Peter might have had to ask forgiveness of the others for denying Christ openly. Some who were more concerned for their own safety than for the well-being of their friends might have had to confess. But when they did, the Day of Pentecost fully came.

So many churches today have lost their power. Their strength has been squandered through internal quarrels and disputes. Their message no longer attracts a hurting world to their doors. Their acts are religious forms rather than living testimonies.

The only way some churches ever expand is when a faction splits from the church because of a disagreement. But churches birthed in hurt will continue to be hurting and ineffective until they are reconciled back to their parents.

As a Christian lawyer, I have been able to work in my own church to help Christians be reconciled to each other.

When people in our church have a dispute with each other, they can contact one of our ministers. The minister then has two laymen work with him on a mediation team to help settle the dispute. ("Where no counsel is, the people fall: but in the multitude of counselers there is safety" [Prov. 11:14].)

The goal is not simply to settle the dispute. It is to bring about healing and restoration between the disputing parties.

When one of our ministers hears of a dispute among members, he sends a letter to the troubled parties, offering reconciliation as a means of settling the dispute and being restored.

In one dispute a Christian businessman outside our local church contacted one of our ministers about a problem he was having. He and a member of our church were in sharp dispute over a business transaction. He wondered if our church could help him settle their differences.

The minister quickly agreed to help. He wrote a letter to the church member, asking him, as a believer in Christ, if he would be willing to accept the church's conciliation services as a means of settling his dispute with his Christian brother.

The church member agreed. Up to this time he and the Christian businessman had not even been talking to each other.

They had both been hurt by a business venture which turned sour. The Christian businessman had supplied the capital for the business, and the member of our church was the comptroller for the business.

As the business continued to operate, it became evident to the comptroller and to other officers of the corporation that the business was under-capitalized and was doomed to failure.

The comptroller and other board members tried to salvage the business and took some "stress money" for their extra efforts.

Meanwhile, the Christian businessman who had supplied the capital was not totally aware of what was happening to the business. He agreed to cover the final salary payments but was unaware of the "stress" payments at the time he announced that decision. He placed some more money in the corporation bank account to cover these salary payments. But the business failed anyway. And, due to the stress payments, one of the comptroller's last salary checks didn't clear the bank because of insufficient funds. The comptroller was extremely angry with the Christian businessman who had funded the business.

And the Christian businessman was angry with him for not explaining the business problems more clearly— like the stress money.

The Christian from our church had even considered filing a civil action against the Christian businessman to recoup his lost salary or report the matter to the state attorney's office for possible criminal action.

When the two Christians came before the conciliation panel, they signed a statement, agreeing to abide by the mediators' decision.

The session opened in prayer, and several verses of Scripture were read, explaining how brothers should be in unity.

Each man was then allowed to present his side of the dispute to the mediators. And while each talked, the Holy Spirit worked in the other's heart, breaking down the walls and hurts which had been separating them. The men started seeing things from the other person's perspective and sensed each other's sincerity.

Finally it was time for the mediation panel to retire and make a decision. The panel sensed a unity in the Spirit and arrived at a decision.

The Christian businessman was to pay the comptroller his final salary minus the amount of the stress money that the comptroller had already received.

The businessman and the comptroller accepted this decision. But more importantly, they once more accepted each other. When they came together, the Holy Spirit had an opportunity to heal their hurts and misunderstandings. They asked each other's forgiveness and were reconciled!

Both men and the mediation panel were deeply moved by the reconciliation experience and discovered how to solve a major problem.

Reconciliation doesn't begin at the headquarters of a denomination. It doesn't start at a national pastor's conference, although it is often needed there. It begins in the heart of each individual believer. Each of us is called to reconciliation, and until believers from the least to the greatest answer that calling, the Church will remain ineffective in winning the world to Christ.

I have to practice reconciliation in my own life more times than I would like to admit. I have had to be reconciled with my wife after I said something wrong or was inconsiderate of her. I have had to apologize to my children when I dominated them instead of loving them. Yes, reconcilation begins in the believer— usually right in his own home.

It is not the easy way out of a problem. But it is God's way. It reaches beyond surface issues to remove roots of bitterness and hurt. It restores people, bringing forgiveness and peace. Let the ministry of reconciliation begin with you today. We can do the healing together.

A Special Note

The author, John Edward Jones, is an active attorney who is involved in the ministry of reconciliation as a layman. He restricts his law practice to the area of personal injury and wrongful death cases and has been designated in this specialty.

All questions and correspondence should be addressed to him as follows:

John Edward Jones, P.A.
P.O. Box 38
Casselberry, FL 32707–0038
(305) 834–5700